ON THE ROOF OF THE WORLD

Around 2:30 A.M., another big avalanche swept by, its wind slashing at our tents. How terrifying an avalanche in the dark can be: the grating, rasping sounds—the blackness. Each avalanche seemed intent on roaring into camp and burying us alive. I would jerk into a sitting position, my eyes wide and searching, expecting to see it burst through the tent walls. I would strain desperately to hear where the cold death was heading, but the sound was deceiving and it was hard to tell where it was. My heart would seemingly stop along with my breathing. We were completely at nature's mercy.

NANDA DEVI

THE TRAGIC EXPEDITION

John Roskelley

AVON BOOKS NEW YORK

AVON BOOKS
A division of
The Hearst Corporation
105 Madison Avenue
New York, New York 10016

Front cover photograph by John P. Evans
Published by arrangement with Stackpole Books
Library of Congress Catalog Card Number: 87-9949
ISBN: 0-380-70568-0

First Avon Books Printing: September 1988

Printed in Canada

UNV 10 9 8 7 6 5 4 3 2

To Joyce,
for giving me the time and support to
pursue my dreams

PREFACE

Nanda Devi, or the "Goddess of Joy" in Hindu mythology, at 25,645 feet is the third highest mountain in the Indian Himalayas. Like a diamond in a cluster of lesser stones, she is surrounded by 18,000- to 22,000-foot peaks. Her slopes drop to the Sanctuary at 14,000 feet, a semilevel area of meadows and flowers, glacial debris, and ice, inhabited only by small herds of Himalayan blue sheep. The only breach in her defense of jagged encircling peaks is the Rishi Gorge, a deep V-shaped canyon several miles long.

While trekking through Northern India in 1949, the American mountaineer Willi Unsoeld spotted Nanda Devi from high on a ridge. Gazing at the mountain, he decided that if he ever had a daughter, she would be named after that magnificent peak. As a mystic, he accepted that his vision of the mountain would hold meaning in his future.

Years later, Willi did have a daughter. Along with her name, he gave to her not only the essence of his past but his hope in the future, when the mountains, inevitably, would fade from his life. As she matured, Devi lived up to her father's expectations. And the desire to see the mountain for which she was named drove her to organize an expedition to climb it.

Devi's image helps soothe the frustration I feel when I try to understand the complexities of the 1976 Indo-American Nanda Devi Expedition, of which I was a member. I began the climb with, who knows, perhaps too much drive and ambition—with an unwavering confidence in my own abilities and my own dreams to fulfill. But it was because of Devi's dreams that eleven men and women challenged the peak Nanda Devi, and her name now summons up in me a quiet strength and conviction. That we found tears on the mountain, instead of joy, is a matter of fate that perhaps only Devi understands.

ONE

My trail to the top of Nanda Devi began in 1975 with a brief letter from Lou Reichardt, my summit partner in 1973 on Nepal's Mt. Dhaulagiri, the world's sixth highest peak. Out of the sixteen mountaineers on the team, Lou and I were the only American members to reach the summit. Even so, I didn't really know him. Like me, Lou doesn't talk much. Thirty-four years old at the time he wrote the note, Lou was a research biophysicist of Einsteinian proportion at the Harvard Medical School. The man I knew from a distance never complained of wind or cold, bad food, or cramped conditions. He carried heavy loads daily and always more than anyone else. He listened and watched carefully from behind heavy black-framed glasses. When he spoke, people listened. He had been particularly intense on Dhaulagiri and was apt to be very quiet at times, creating uneasy silences. Lou was there to summit perhaps partly in memory of seven companions who had died on Dhaulagiri in 1969. When an ice avalanche appeared out of the fog, he had been the only one to survive.

His letter to me was direct. "John: You have been invited to join Ad Carter's expedition to Nanda Devi next summer. Can you go? Get back to me ASAP. Lou."

I remembered one photo of the 25,645-foot peak from Tilman and Odell's *On Top of the World*, the story of the first ascent in 1936. The photo showed Nanda Devi rising almost twelve thousand feet from the floor of the "Sanctuary." White-capped, steep, with incredibly long, sharp ridges, not another peak within a hundred square miles could match its grandeur. The difficulty of a major expedition in such a remote area had worried me slightly at the time and I felt apprehensive. But I would have gone anywhere in the world to be on another expedition. Expeditions were like candy to me; I couldn't seem to get enough. I didn't really care what mountain it was or how high.

At the time of Lou's note, I had been climbing eleven years. I had reached the summit of Dhaulagiri with Lou in 1973, was a member of the first American climbing team to Russia in 1974, and had climbed the North Face of the Eiger on the way home from Russia—Chris Kopczynski and I were the first all-American team to do so. (Only one other American had climbed the face and he had been with a German.) I made a significant first-ascent route in Bolivia and many Grade VIs and Vs in the United States and Canada. I could hardly be called physically impressive with my small-boned, although muscular, five-foot ten-inch frame, but I had proven my strength and tenacity on several of the hardest climbs in the world. I was strong, but so are many others who participate in sports. The difference was that I didn't know I could be beaten.

My reputation as a mountaineer must have persuaded Ad Carter to invite me to join the expedition. No doubt Lou's recommendation helped relieve Ad's fears about my other reputation, as one who questioned authority.

"We want to try a new route on the north side," Lou explained over the telephone, "possibly hitting the North Ridge around 21,000 feet and following it to the summit. The only pictures we have of the upper five thousand feet are pretty vague and we don't have any shots taken from the Sanctuary floor."

"How do you know there is a reasonable route?"

"Ad seems to remember the northwest side looking feasible, at least to the ridge."

"Who are the other team members?"

"Willi Unsoeld is a coleader with Ad."

In 1976, Ad Carter was a language teacher at a private school in Boston. He had been a member of the 1936 Nanda Devi team that had made the first ascent and would organize and colead the current expedition. A distinguished Bostonian whose strongest word under stress is "damn," he was invaluable to any expedition for his experience. At sixty-two, Ad was still game to trek into the remote mountain ranges of the world. My contact with him had been through the *American Alpine Journal*, which he has edited for many years. From our correspondence I knew him as decisive and to the point.

Willi Unsoeld, then forty-nine, was one of the American climbers I knew from reputation: he was a mountaineering legend. At that time he was a professor of religion at Evergreen State College in Washington. I had read several books on his and Horbein's ascent of the West Ridge of Mt. Everest in 1963 and was awed by their undertaking. Willi was known as easygoing and lovable, but his ascents revealed a steel will. I had climbed several of Willi's routes on peaks throughout the U.S. and found them to be beautiful and difficult. He was a solid all-around mountaineer.

"What a great pair to lead an expedition," I said. "Who else?"

"Willi's daughter, Devi, who is kind of the instigator of the trip, and his son, Krag," replied Lou.

"Have they ever been to altitude?"

"Some, while they were living in Nepal."

"Have they done much climbing?"

Lou hestitated. "Well, of sorts with Willi in the Tetons and the Cascades." He then named several climbers who were well known to me because of our association on other expeditions.

"It sounds to me like we need a few more technical climbers, Lou. Who else has been invited?"

"Well, you know John Evans. He will try and make it after his wife has their baby."

I knew from the Russian Pamirs expedition that John Evans was strong. He had completed significant ascents in Alaska, Antarctica, Russia, and the U.S. Evans was then thirty-seven and program director for the Colorado Outward Bound School. A big man of herculean strength, he could carry the heaviest loads, hour after hour, showing little fatigue. John's greatest contribution to an expedition was his leadership. I immediately assumed that he would be the team's climbing leader on the mountain.

"Ad has also asked Elliot Fisher, who has climbed in South America with him," Lou continued. Elliot, a tall, lanky medical student of twenty-three, had several first ascents on peaks located in the Cordilleras of Peru. He had a wonderful sense of humor and was eager to participate on major expeditions. Ad had been very impressed with Elliot's ability in Peru and was pleased to have him along.

Lou was concerned about being pressured to add another woman. Expedition member Peter Lev had asked the leaders if Marty Hoey, a strong mountaineer and his live-in partner, could join the team. Willi had been particularly enthusiastic over this arrangement. Lou didn't like the idea and my first reaction was the same. Marty was as strong as any of the men climbers mentioned, as she had shown in the Russian Pamirs, but we felt it would be best not to include two individuals, like Peter and Marty, who were living together. Their reactions to each other could diminish their concentration and commitment to the climb. Lou would pass our opinions on to Ad.

Lou asked me to recommend a doctor who could join the expedition, and I immediately thought of Jim States. Every climb we had done together had been a major first ascent, including several we had completed in Bolivia less than two weeks before. Jim seemed possessed of energy without a way to cap it. Hard work and long hours as director of Spokane's methadone program during the week never stopped him from throwing an oversize pack on his back and going as far and fast as he could during his days off. Behind the curly red hair and beard were sparkling eyes and a warm smile that revealed kindness and good humor, bringing out the best of those around him. It didn't take long for him to accept, and a week later he was an official member of the team.

The expedition to Nanda Devi had been conceived by Nanda Devi Unsoeld while she was visiting Ad Carter and his wife at their Boston home. She proposed ascending the peak by a new route and led by Ad to commemorate

Willi, as a last resort, came up with the only other reasoning we hadn't dared mention.

"Let's use the Nanda Devi Expedition to show that men and women can do this sort of thing together without problems," he said.

Suddenly aware that I was standing in the way of a great American experiment, I grudgingly conceded.

"Hell, it hasn't ever worked before. What makes you think it's going to work now?"

But they were not quite through. In the next half hour, Willi had persuaded me to call Marty and ask her to reconsider.

The three of us discussed other major differences that had cropped up during the preceding months. I was astonished at the gap between us on such important issues as style of ascent, use of fixed lines, and type of food. Peter seemed to want to climb Nanda Devi in a day, alpine style, with a minimum of food and equipment. Willi preferred more variety of food and equipment but liked the idea of an alpine-style ascent. With the size of our team and an as-yet-unknown route—we didn't even have a good picture—I had figured on using the traditional Himalayan method, establishing camps and fixing lines to facilitate carrying loads. We wisely left the decisions for the team meeting in Issaquah, Washington, in December.

Just before dinner, Devi swept in like a small tornado after an obviously brutal game of soccer with some friends from Evergreen State College. Her warm smile and casual appearance were relaxing. I could tell she was confident and a real competitor. But her confidence began to disturb me as the evening progressed and our conversation centered on the expedition. Devi had spent seven years of her youth in Nepal, where she had learned to speak Nepali fluently. Her experience as a climber was limited. She believed mountains were more to feel from the heart and touch with the eyes than to tread with the feet. Her opinions on the major issues were not being based on experience, but idealistic emotions. I liked her, though. She was fresh, exuberant, alive, and she would add these qualities to the team.

Meanwhile, Krag seemed cautious and quiet, almost to the point of being unfriendly. He seemed to be protecting his territory from a stranger, in this case—me. He outlined the purpose of the expedition: in his eyes, this would be a family trek and an opportunity to explore a new area. I found it hard to believe the climb was not important to him. My interest in going only to reach the summit must have irritated him because neither of us said more than a few words to the other again. Later, while on the mountain, Willi confided to Jim States that this conversation had been the main reason Krag later decided not to join the expedition.

I drove back to my hotel questioning the true nature of the expedition for the first time. Was this really supposed to be a "family style" expedition? Picking a team is the most important aspect of an expedition. Each mountain has difficulties, challenges, dangers, and problems that require different personalities and skills. I study the route first when I choose a team. Each one is complex and unique. When I know the intricacies of the route, then I pick a team capable of handling its problems. Each climber becomes a piece in a three-dimensional puzzle. Each must adapt quickly to a changing environment; their abilities must be broad and sharply honed for the type of route to be climbed.

The Nanda Devi team was chosen more by acquaintance than by particular needs. This method—joining because of who you know rather than by what you know—is by far the more common in climbing. Often it lessens the expedition's chances for success.

I called Marty as I told Willi and Peter I would. She sounded half asleep. She was quite convinced she was not wanted, and, figuratively speaking, I was wearing out the knees on my pants when she finally agreed to go on the expedition. Relieved that I would not have to tell Willi that I had failed to convince her to go on the trip, I chatted on aimlessly.

"How are you and Peter doing?" I asked.

"Well, John, I'm trying to break up with him slowly right now so as not to hurt him. I want to be back on my own."

My worst fears were now reality. I couldn't help remembering Peter's assurance that he and Marty were "inseparable." Peter was in love and this was going to devastate him to the point of being useless on the expedition. I hoped that Marty would let him down easy.

The first official team meeting was held in Issaquah, Washington, during the 1975 American Alpine Club annual meeting in December. Five of us, plus a few friends and family, were in attendance. Ad began passing out fuzzy pictures of our intended route and maps of the area to Willi, Devi, Elliot, and me. Chris Bonington's picture, taken from Changabang, one of the Sanctuary peaks, showed the upper three thousand feet of the route, but the photo had been taken from such a distance that it was of little use. One thing the picture did make clear: between approximately 22,000 and 24,000 feet was an ominous rock buttress rising vertically from a knifelike ridge crest. There seemed to be no reasonable alternative other than to confront this problem head-on, a very difficult task at that altitude. The bottom eight thousand feet of our intended route remained completely unknown.

Having determined as much of the route as we could, the problems of logistics and itinerary were next. It immediately became obvious that the expedition was composed of two factions: those who wanted to climb Nanda Devi alpine style, and those who thought it better—with a team of thirteen climbers—to use the traditional Himalayan method.

Peter, Willi, Marty, and Devi had become the strongest advocates of an alpine-style ascent. This style was becoming more popular in the Himalayas but was used primarily by two- or four-person teams of very experienced climbers with equal ability. The style necessitates a quick burst from a very low camp, with the climbers carrying everything with them in order to keep moving up for several days, until the summit is reached. The dangers are obvious. A storm could cut off retreat for days, even weeks. High-altitude illnesses would be fatal without the backup of bottled oxygen. Rescue in almost every circumstance would be impossible except by the injured or ill climber's teammates, who could very well be in the same condition. The alpine style's advantages include less time spent at altitude, fewer carries across dangerous slopes in the path of rockfall or avalanches, and, in the purest sense, a cleaner style of climb, one that is less dependent on an umbilical cord of supplies.

The traditional Himalayan method would mean a slower, more cumbersome expedition, but a much better chance of success. Camp after camp would be established and stocked with the equipment and food needed for future camps above. Fixed line between them would assure retreat and safeguard the climbers as they carried daily loads. The summit could be reached from the last camp in a day by well-acclimatized climbers. The dangers of such a method are a little more subtle. The climbers are exposed to potential avalanche, ice falls, and rockfall for a much longer time. Illnesses that would not be detrimental during an alpine-style ascent, such as coughs, infections, severe diarrhea, and general high-altitude lethargy, can become serious, even deadly, during extended periods of altitude. Lou, Jim, and I, although usually advocates of alpine-style climbing, were hoping that with thirteen climbers, some inexperienced at high altitude and of differing abilities, the team would accept the traditional style. But if it had been just Lou, Jim, and me, we would definitely have taken the alpine-style approach.

The amount of fixed rope that should be taken became a critical issue for both factions. Neither wanted to admit defeat so early in the meeting. The traditional method required a considerable amount of fixed line; the alpine method didn't need it. The issue was finally dropped after we tentatively agreed that the expedition would take four thousand feet of rope, including the eleven millimeter lead-climbing ropes. Lou and I figured the four thousand feet was only half of what was needed for a team the size of ours.

The discussion went from rope to food, easing the tension somewhat. Food is the single most important item on any climb, whether in the Cascades of Washington or the Himalayas of Asia. It is particularly important to long-term expeditions where climbers spend months on a mountain putting up with numerous daily inconveniences. Every climber hopes that the food on an expedition will be nourishing and even tasty.

Each voiced his opinion on what food to take and how much. Peter wanted to eat only Indian food on the mountain (his alpine-style ascent would suffer from the weight of cabbages, raw goat meat, and unleavened bread). I preferred to eat freeze-dried meals during the trek in and climb (despite the noxious gas produced from freeze-dried meals). Ad wanted to eat only basic foods, such as oatmeal, "as we did in 1936." We compromised, agreeing to eat Indian food on the trek and mostly freeze-dried meals on the climb. Ad took charge of menus and quantities. No one questioned his ability to do a superb job, although he was known on occasion to take too little of some important foods. With any luck, oatmeal would be the one commodity he forgot.

Our meeting finally ended late in the afternoon. Every issue had been discussed, from date of departure to the addition of toilet tissue. (The latter had been quite controversial. Born and bred an environmentalist, Devi thought it ridiculous to take toilet tissue on the expedition. I made a mental note to add six rolls to my travel bag, just in case she won the argument.)

We had accomplished a great deal under the circumstances and departed feeling good toward one another. There were many loose ends yet to tie up, but we felt they would get done in the seven months left before departure. I couldn't understand why Willi, considering his experience, was backing Devi and Peter on some of their ideas. One thing became clear. The two opposing factions had to reach some type of understanding before leaving for India.

During the next few months, the members exchanged letters ranging from Ad's informing each individual of his responsibilities to my reports on donated equipment. In early March 1976, Lou, Ad, and their wives began packing the two tons of gear that had accumulated in Ad's basement.

A typical packing session was slightly chaotic and

completely understaffed, as Lou described it. He became quite worried that Ad was underestimating the amount of food the team would need and not packing enough. He did not want to upset Ad, but he felt the situation was critical. So as telephone calls and short errands took Ad away from the basement, Lou and his wife, Kathy, would stuff partly filled boxes with extra freeze-dried food and drink mix, seal the boxes permanently, and stack them with the finished loads. Upon Ad's return, they would be packing the new box with equipment designated to go. The system worked so well that Lou was soon beefing up the fixed-rope allotment as well. It seemed all the issues that had created so many differences in the team were finally being resolved.

Prior to our departure, Lou fell while rock climbing and injured the ligaments in both shoulders. He expected surgery and informed Ad that he wouldn't be going to Nanda Devi. Willi, however, wouldn't let him give up so easily. Lou soon began physical therapy instead of having surgery, and, to everyone's relief, he improved sufficiently to join the team again. The only problem was that he would have to join us in India several weeks late.

Marty, Willi, and I boarded the transcontinental flight to New York's Kennedy Airport in Seattle on July 5, 1976, according to schedule. We met several of the other members in New York; the rest would meet in India. I felt good recounting old times with Marty. Her job as a guide on Mt. Rainier had put steel springs in her legs and adorned her face with an attractive tan. I was glad, after all, that she was going.

Willi was lighthearted and eager. We discussed a mountaineering lawsuit in which he and I were both serving as expert witnesses. We laughed and kidded each other for taking opposite views again, a situation that had become quite apparent during the last six months.

New York was stifling under a midseason heat wave. To save money, we shouldered heavy packs and walked to the international-terminal building several blocks away. We were the first of our group to arrive, but not by long. Jim States, loaded down with eighty pounds of medical gear plus his own personal equipment, soon entered the Air India lounge.

Jim was incredibly happy. He had just spent three days with his entire family in Pittsburgh for the first time in many years. He felt a closeness to his father and sister that he had never before experienced and when the time had come to leave it had been very difficult. Now he faced the adventure of his life.

Peter and team member Andy Harvard arrived within minutes of each other. Peter, quaking with excitement to be on his way again, checked his baggage and joined Marty in the upstairs lounge.

Andy Harvard, a twenty-seven-year-old law student, was a cautious, deliberate mountaineer and adventurer. He had been a member of the 1973 Dhaulagiri Expedition and was a veteran of several trips to Alaska and South America. Quiet and patient, with a deep resonant voice, he commanded attention when he offered his opinion. Andy seemed able to relax his lanky six-foot frame under any circumstances. He had a suntanned face set beneath black beard and scraggly hair. I often noticed a faraway look in his dark brown eyes. Andy's excuse to travel foreign lands was climbing and, although short on technical ability, he added to any team because of experience.

Andy seemed unusually quiet and I felt that I hardly knew him, even after the three months we had spent together on the Dhaulagiri expedition. Just before departure, Andy and I had a beer in the lounge. He was, as usual, very sincere. He didn't feel like going on the expedition and still wasn't sure why he was there. Andy mentioned that he had just broken up with a woman he was quite fond of and didn't have his equilibrium back yet. Our conversation ended abruptly as our flight was called.

As we took our seats in the Air India 747, I felt calm and relaxed for the first time in months. The problems the team had faced in organizing the expedition were far from my thoughts. It was time for us to work toward a common goal—to climb Nanda Devi.

TWO

The sun was low in the east as we arrived at New Delhi International Airport. Although it was still early morning, a muggy blast of monsoon heat pushed its way into the plane's cabin as the doors opened. Shuttle buses took us and the other weary tourists to the terminal building and Indian Customs. The large propeller fans that were rotating lazily overhead epitomized the apathetic, inefficient Indian bureaucracy. Willi, who spoke some Hindi, breezed by without a second look from his customs officer, but another officer detected a slight flaw in one of our group's visa application. Each of us was singled out and our passports taken. They required a search of our personal belongings. I had gone through this scene many times before and invariably the customs officer thinks he has captured an American agent. Why else would I be carrying pitons, carabiners, and my jumars—a handled contraption used to ascend ropes that has a toothed gate and a trigger mechanism?

The inspector finally smiled, satisfied that he had done his duty, and stamped my passport. I managed to stuff most of the seventy-five pounds of gear back into my carry-on pack, shoulder the rest, and head for the door. Outside, the flies and local bag boys descended on me. We were in India.

Ad and his wife Ann, Devi, and Elliot were waiting for us in the passenger pick-up area. This was the kind of individual effort that would enhance a strong team. Jim was introduced to those team members he didn't know and the rest of us greeted one another warmly. Ad filled us in on the progress he had made with the Indian Mountaineering Federation (IMF).

"We are going to have two strong Indian climbers with us," Ad said. "Captain Kiran Kumar, who was on Bonington's Changabang Expedition, and Sergeant Nirmal Singh, an instructor of mountaineering. We'll meet Kumar this afternoon, Nirmal we'll meet at Joshimath."

This was welcome news for several reasons. First, Indian climbers could perform the same functions as would a liaison officer, an official usually appointed by the Indian government, but paid and equipped by the expedition, to accompany the climbers from Base Camp until completion of the expedition. Liaison officers could be quite annoying if they demanded procedure be followed to the letter. The expedition needs the liaison's permission to change routes or departure dates. Most liaisons preferred the comfort of an office in New Delhi to living on the side of a mountain. Kiran and Nirmal, however, were reputed to be strong, experienced Himalayan mountaineers. Furthermore, Kiran had served as liaison officer for the 1974 Changabang Expedition, which followed the same trek we were to make.

Second, the IMF would donate fifteen hundred dollars for each of the two Indians, the amount each of us had put into the expedition. They would also supply several IMF trainees to work as high-altitude porters, one of whom would be our cook. The expedition would equip them and pay the standard wage to each.

From the airport, our taxi driver weaved in and out of traffic, giving the numerous holy cattle wide berths and the ragged street urchins narrow escapes, en route to New Delhi's YMCA, one of the capital city's more modern hotels. The thick, one-hundred-degree heat devouring New Delhi was a prelude to the monsoon, which was several weeks late.

Rooms had been reserved for each two individuals. Jim and I signed the register, grabbed our gear, and walked upstairs to wash off the accumulations of two days' travel. I began to feel civil again. After a continental lunch in the YMCA dining room, Ad asked everyone to his room for a meeting.

"The IMF has asked me if we would like an army transmitter and a two-man crew to run it at Base Camp," he said. "Does anyone feel we need them?" Our response was unanimously negative. Ad then passed out travel permits and visa extension forms, which we filled in while Jim covered the medical problems that we could encounter during the trek in and at altitude. I was reminded with all this that an expedition is ninety percent business and ten percent active sport.

Medical briefings are a prerequisite to all major expeditions because too often a doctor can't get to the sick or injured climber. The treatment and care for the victim must be given by a fellow climber who is at hand. Each climber learns the symptoms and treatment for high-altitude problems such as pulmonary edema, cerebral edema, and acute mountain sickness. A proper diagnosis by a layman in the early stages of an illness at altitude can save the victim's life.

"I suggest we all start using very careful hygiene habits to prevent any sickness from spreading," Jim requested. "That means using your own cup, water bottle, and silverware. We should all start using iodine in the water to prevent dysentery, too. Everyone agree?" We did, after protests over the bad taste iodine left in the mouth.

Ad informed us that the equipment shipped by freighter from Boston in March had arrived in New Delhi and was now being transported to the YMCA for repacking. We were scheduled to leave New Delhi on the night of July 9, giving us two days to complete the packing.

At dinner that evening, Captain Kiran Inder Kumar, a thirty-one-year-old parachute commando for an elite regiment in the Indian Army, was introduced to us. Captain Kumar would oversee government regulations and transportation problems, hire porters, purchase food and, in general, move the expedition like a troop column through northern India to the base of Nanda Devi. I couldn't imagine a more qualified man to do it. Ten years of rigorous army discipline gave the meticulously groomed Kiran a king's posture and a wrestler's muscles. Kiran had been on four major expeditions and had led the 1973 Indian-Bhutan Gong Kar Expedition. His last expedition had been to Changabang in 1974 with Bonington where he had taken a serious fall, injured his shoulder, and been unable to participate on the summit climb. Although he still lacked confidence in the shoulder, he was determined to make an all-out effort on Nanda Devi. His clear, bell-like tenor flagged our attention whenever he spoke. He had a stubbly start of a beard overshadowed by a thick, unruly handlebar moustache and dark brown eyes that always seemed to be smiling.

The next morning we faced repacking the gear. Ad had requisitioned the YMCA's enclosed backyard for the newly arrived equipment crates, now stacked like building blocks. Elliot, who had the only master list of the contents of each container, tried to organize us into work details to perform specific functions. Each porter load had to be under sixty pounds and no load could contain the expedition's total amount of an item should a load be lost, stolen, or dropped into a river during the trek in. During the 1936 Nanda Devi Expedition, a porter slipped while traversing the Rishi Gorge and lost his load into the river far below. The load contained all the crampons for the climbers. Luckily, the climbers had tricouni nails on their climbing boots, which substituted nicely in the deep monsoon snows.

We began opening boxes, separating the equipment into piles, packaging perishable foods and clothing in plastic bags, weighing the finished loads, and restacking them. Cold Cokes and *Limcas*—an Indian soft drink—quenched our ever-present thirst. The sun took its toll. Individuals would disappear for hours, leaving the few diehards behind to take up the slack. Any organization we had soon evaporated.

The most tedious and demanding job became untangling the six-hundred-foot spools of rope that had broken open during shipment from Germany. It required hours of threading, pulling, and winding the ten thousand feet of rope. Each six-hundred-foot length was then cut in half, coiled, and packed away. Several thousand feet of rope that Jim, Ad, and I couldn't sneak into more loads were left unpacked in New Delhi on the insistence of the alpine-style advocates.

The following morning, July 9, most of us dug away at the mountain of equipment still left to repack before our departure that evening. The dead air in the courtyard was like a sauna. Beads of sweat clung to my brow only to splatter on the waterproof cardboard packing boxes and sizzle. One after another, team members took shelter from the sun and disappeared to their rooms. The master list of the contents of each box became a scribbled, careless mess. I had to raise my voice so I could be heard over the buzzing of the multitude of flies that swarmed around us, an indication we smelled worse than the cow dung that paved New Delhi's streets. The flies attacked so mercilessly that I felt beaten into punch-drunk submission by the end of the day.

Devi seemed untouched by the heat and the pests. She would look at me as if to say, "Tired, John?" and smile, lifting another sixty-pound box over her head to the top of the stack. Devi seemed vibrant, alive, happy to be in India and close to her namesake. While in New Delhi, she had drawn significant interest from the Indian news media for her participation in the climb.

"I feel a very close relationship with Nanda Devi," she told an *Indian Times* reporter who interviewed her. "I can't describe it, but there has been something within me about this mountain ever since I was born." Her dream, like that of her father, was to reach the summit of Nanda Devi.

I kept wondering if she would ever take a break, even a short breather, and rest. About the only fatigue she showed was a hoarse cough, one that she and Elliot had picked up several weeks before in Nepal. It would linger for some time.

The leaders felt it was up to each person to decide what his or her role would be during the trip. To me, this meant they did not want to give direct orders or force someone to do a job. This put responsibility on each of us. Some members accepted this better than others. Peter, however, was taking full advantage of the circumstances. He could be found permanently attached to his bed, a human blanket, ignoring our half-hearted harassment to come help us. Team spirit can be built by overcoming difficulties together on or off the mountain. That spirit is the key to success on a large expedition, but it wasn't happening here.

The mildew green lorry, rented to transport the expedition to Rishikesh, 120 miles northeast, arrived promptly at nine o'clock that night. One by one we gathered in the courtyard to pack our two tons of gear into the antique diesel Tata truck. Leftover group equipment and personal gear was dumped into an empty hotel room to be collected and stored by our travel agents. Friends and well wishers gathered behind the vehicle as we said our good-byes and good lucks. Ad spent the last few moments hugging his wife Ann, who had originally intended to accompany the expedition to Base Camp, but had injured her back. With her index finger, Kiran's young wife, Rama, placed a red *tilak* on each of our foreheads for good luck. His two young sons passed around pastries as we clambered aboard to find a comfortable spot to spend the next two days.

I squirmed into the compartment over the cab with the tarps, spare tire, toolbox, and grease. The shimmering heat of the day was gone, replaced by a cool breeze, the prelude to an approaching storm. Devi, Jim, and Elliot lay flat on the rain tarp, which was stretched taut and tied over the fence-like railing that encircled the truck bed. Jim pulled part of the tarp over them as a blanket and tied a rope over them all so they could not roll off in their sleep.

Short squalls of warm rain periodically cleansed our faces of road dust and the diesel fumes from other trucks that passed in the dark. Kiran handled checkpoints, which became increasingly frequent, and whose officers became more suspicious. His Hindi rose in pitch as he became sleepier and less tolerant of the inquisitive guards. I thought his patience was astounding.

We followed the leveed sides of the Ganges through the holy city of Hardwar. At daybreak we rolled into the foothills of the Himalayas. Rishikesh, its crowded streets bustling with daily activity, received only a few yawns and sleepy glances. We continued on several miles outside of town to wait for a different truck. Kiran returned to

Rishikesh to check on the truck while most of the team slept. Jim and I flipped a Frisbee about and managed to interest a young Indian boy in the game.

An hour later Kiran returned and informed us that we had made a mistake, the truck was waiting for us in the city. We piled aboard our truck and soon were in Rishikesh. We hadn't eaten, or quenched our thirst, for some time, and several fruit stands were a short distance away. A six-year-old waif sold me several tangerines, cleaning each with her tattered dress as if it were a precious stone.

Jim was interested in the local practice of medicine and ducked into a small room designated by a picture sign. I followed and was introduced by Jim as, "My intern, Mr. Roskelley." One professional-looking gentleman in the typical baggy white pants bartered for our cameras. After we refused to sell he took us to an outpatient clinic. The "physician" told Jim about the miracle cures he had performed for serious illnesses with the use of certain herbs. We politely refused one of his concoctions and left.

Several of us had a street tailor make loose pajamas for trekking pants, a comfortable way to dress in the Indian heat. While they were being made, Jim and I hunted down umbrellas for everyone and two snow shovels for the mountain. Four youths approached as we bartered for the goods.

"You climb Nanda Devi?" one smiling youth asked.

"Why, yes. Well, we intend to try," Jim answered. "How did you know?"

They all laughed as the one boy whipped from behind his back a copy of the *Indian Times*, which sported a black-and-white photo of the team and a brief article. The boy pointed out the two of us in the photo.

Roaring with laughter, Jim couldn't believe we were already celebrities, even in remote northern India. We gathered up our purchases and returned to our new vehicle, a brightly painted truck with yellow, red, and green flowers decorating the bumpers and cab.

Permit stations and army checkpoints slowed our progress. Our truck climbed slowly along the Ganges, leaving the pallid, flat Indian farmland behind for the forested gorges and sharp ridges of the foothills. The driver's expertise became apparent as he snaked the truck through the countless hairpins and corners that cut the gorge wall. Driver warnings painted on large boulders and road-cut walls in English and Hindi in red lettering over bright yellow paint said, *Honk, Please*, or *Slow Down!* Around the corner another rock would say, *Thank You*. My perch from the top of the truck gave me an eagle's eye view of the Hindu temples and ashrams—lodging houses for pilgrims—that lined the banks of the Ganges below.

Thirty miles from Rishikesh we entered Devapryog, where the confluence of two great rivers, the Bhagirathi and Alaknanda, unite to form the Ganges, which then flows over fifteen hundred miles to the sea. Hundreds of top-knotted sadhus thronged the bathing steps that descended into the two rivers, many anchored to chains while they bathed in the holy water to keep from being swept away in the strong current. Laboring porters, the veins puffing in their necks and muscular legs, were straining under 176-pound sacks of *atta* (Indian wheat flour) en route to market.

Our driver ground down the gears as we descended to the Bhagirathi Ganga, crossed on the recently constructed bridge, and pursued the northern reaches of the Alaknanda. We gained height again quickly, weaving through the terraced fields and lush forests alive with langur monkeys. Land sluffs and mud slides commonly destroyed sections of the road and we were forced to detour around work crews who took days to repair by hand a stretch that would have taken hours by machine in the United States.

We were starting to feel the effects of the long road journey that we had undertaken without food or drink since Rishikesh. A dinner halt was finally ordered late in the evening at Srinigar, a small village. Most of us ordered Cokes, fried meats, and pastries with rice. Only Willi and Devi were able to down the cold greasy meal blanketed by green flies. After several bites I walked across the street to purchase Himalayan-brand sugar cookies, the mainstay of the local traveler. Willi finished his meal and concentrated on cleaning up the others' leftovers.

"What's wrong with you guys?" Willi asked, his eyes laughing. "This is the best meal I've had in days."

We all looked at each other, making various faces of disgust. Jim muttered something about keeping his guts in one piece. Marty, who had stayed on the truck, refused any tea or food, which at the time was quite reasonable. She and several of the others were beginning to show some travel sickness. Craving sleep, I wasn't too enthused about continuing.

I found a flat empty spot beneath the tarp as we traveled on, but the trip continued to be annoyingly rocky and, because of the diesel fumes, slightly nauseating. Around 2:00 A.M., after no sleep for thirty hours, I had had it. My nerves were shot. This nonstop traveling was insane. The whole team was being physically weakened and several members were becoming ill, but no one would give up this "tough it out" attitude that seemed to preclude common sense. Neither did I like making a commotion over a problem that should have been solved beforehand. We were taking a chance with everyone's health by not stopping to sleep or eat properly. Crawling to the back of the truck, I found Willi.

"Willi! Hey, Willi!"

"Yeah, what is it, John?" he answered sleepily.

"Willi, dammit, why aren't we stopping to sleep? This truck has got to stop now and let all of us get some rest. We're going to be physical wrecks before we start into the peak. I'm going to have the truck pull over now."

"O.K., O.K., take it easy," Willi said. "I'll get out and tell the driver to pull over at the next stop."

Our relief was overwhelming after we stopped. For five hours we slept without diesel fumes, swaying, dust, or grinding gears. Everyone seemed refreshed in the morning, although famished. We passed through Chomoli at daybreak and were in Joshimath, the "county seat" of Uttar Pradesh, before 10:00 A.M.

Joshimath, a steep terraced village of whitewashed buildings with slate-shingled roofs, was located two thousand feet above the swift Alaknanda River. Thousand-foot walls bordered the village on two sides. Kiran located several rooms for the night in the Himalayan Hotel, one of the newer establishments in town.. We unloaded our personal gear from the truck, feeling refreshed in the cool air of 6,000 feet. Accompanied by Ad and Willi, Kiran disappeared: passports had to be cleared, trekking permits issued, food purchased, and Nirmal Singh, our second Indian teammate, located. Nirmal was to be in Joshimath early to hire porters.

The rest of us took cold showers, washed clothes, and caught up on our diaries. Jim and I shouldered our cameras and sauntered up the street to photograph the vitality of this Garhwali village. We were encircled immediately by youngsters in school uniform who tested their newly acquired foreign language on us. "What time is it?" they yelled in flawless English, reaching for my wrist to look for themselves because they didn't understand my answer. Teasing, I would hold out my digital Pulsar, among the first of its kind, and delight in their bewilderment at a watch with no face. When I pushed the button and the time lit up, they would gasp and draw back. Meanwhile, Jim was taking some fine photographic portraits.

Late in the afternoon we walked back to the hotel to find the rest of the team at the Himalayan Restaurant, waiting for their ordered dinners. A green-turbaned Sikh resembling the actor Omar Sharif stood beside Kiran at the dinner table.

Willi introduced Jim and me to Sergeant Nirmal Singh, a high-altitude warfare instructor for the Indian Army and our second Indian teammate. Nirmal would be in charge of transport logistics, the high-altitude porters, and would help Kiran get the expedition to Base Camp and climb Nanda Devi.

Nirmal, thirty-two, had been in the army fifteen years and was considered one of the army's most qualified mountaineering instructors. Nirmal had been on one expedition to Kashmir, where he climbed 19,000-foot Kola Hoi. He busied himself during his time off from the army on his farm, where he had a wife and two children.

His English was broken and seldom used, but much better than our Hindi.

I immediately took to Nirmal's playful zest for life. Ten minutes after I met him, he had me in front of the mirror, putting on his turban to the laughter of several Indians standing nearby. Here, I thought, is the man I will probably summit with if he is as good as they say. I was pleased that our team had been strengthened by this new addition.

The Himalayan Hotel's food was sickeningly similar to Srinigar's—a cold, foul-smelling rice-and-egg dish swarming with flies. I had a touch of diarrhea and ate very little that night, although I did drink pot after pot of hot tea. I made the mistake of entering the kitchen after dinner and wished I hadn't. The smoky, dirt-floored room received water from a common village stream that was running through the building in a floor gutter. The water came from much higher where each household used it first, not only for drinking, but for cleaning purposes, even sewage. Dogs snatched at the scraps littering the floor and one cur sprawled among the vegetables. The cook looked like a beggar but wasn't quite as clean. He evidently had the family in for the night because there were two older people sitting on bed-like cots. Naked children played in and around the stored food. They all had terrible deep coughs and running noses, very common problems in the Garhwal. Smoke from the chimneyless cook fire smothered the small room. My eyes were beginning to burn and water by the time I had seen enough and ducked out the tiny door.

So as not to ruin the appetites of the others, I failed to mention my kitchen visit, pretending during the next few meals to be full from eating so much while in the village.

We returned to our rooms for the night to find one too many people for the number of beds. Elliot graciously sacked out on the floor. I called his attention to an enormous willow-legged spider directly overhead.

"Look at his eyes, Elliot . . . I think he's watching you."

"Yeah, Elliot," Andy continued, "Brute, up there, doesn't like people on his floor."

"Well, Brute will have to live with it," Elliot joked, and shut off the light. After five more minutes of kidding in the dark, Elliot switched on the light again. To our surprise, Brute the spider was down the wall, only a foot from Elliot's sleeping bag. With a loud whack of his tennis shoe, he made Brute a permanent fixture on the wall. We spent the rest of the night in peaceful slumber.

I awoke the next morning, July 12, to the constant hammering of the pull-cord on the standup toilet. Many of the team, including Jim and me, were suffering from some degree of diarrhea. Those who had been eating the local food had it worse. Whatever the cause, toilet tissue became a much-desired commodity even for those who thought it ridiculous before the trip began.

Nevertheless, Jim, Marty, and I set out to explore the far reaches of the village. The all-too-common smell of human waste intensified along the streets, where gutters oozed blackish alkaline sewer waste from the center of the village. We picked a rock outcrop on the far end of the village to watch several pairs of Himalayan golden eagles glide and drift on the updrafts created by the warming of the air in the deep gorge of the river. Effortlessly, one soared along the rim, occasionally circling and rising on a warm air current, only to float away again in search of prey. Later, Jim wanted to visit the village hospital to get an idea of the porter illnesses he would have to treat. Marty was particularly enthusiastic, so we broke away from the eagles and followed the red crosses painted conspicuously on boulders along a narrow road.

We stopped in front of the head office and after a brief sign-language encounter with a staff officer, were escorted into the army commandant's office. He was far from pleasant and eyed all of us with distrust. He became quite defensive about Jim's medical questions, wondering why we would come to an army hospital for such information. Jim finally got the hint and we departed with a very cool good-bye.

With business in town completed at 5:00 P.M., we loaded our personal gear into the truck and started for Lata, only twelve miles distant but hours away. Half a mile into town we stopped to pick up the porters and trek food of *atta*, *daal*, rice, sugar, tea, *ghee*, assorted spices, and plenty of cigarettes for the porters. Nirmal was accompanied by two of the Mountaineering Institute trainees who would serve as high-altitude porters—Jatendra and Surrendra—who, along with several other local Indians who had been promised jobs, climbed aboard the overloaded vehicle.

Kiran worked feverishly to free us quickly at each of the three checkpoints within a mile of town. Before long we crossed a recently built iron bridge and turned at right angles to a cliff onto a steep hill. The heavily laden diesel couldn't pull the grade. We jumped off and waited while the driver backed up, gunned the overworked engine, and made a run for it. The truck just couldn't do it.

We unloaded the 176-pound bags of food and carried them to the top of the hill. Nirmal insisted on carrying each bag alone, while the Americans decided teamwork offered less pain. I took Nirmal's challenge, loaded a sack of *atta* on my back, and made a dash for the top. The whoops and hollers from my compatriots didn't ease the load as my leg muscles jellied and the load slipped forward over the top of my head. My pride hurt worse than my burlap-burned ear or back. The half-loaded truck managed, with only inches to spare, to make the hill. We threw everything back into a disorganized mess and continued on our way.

The night took us through the village of Reni, and we stopped at a postage-stamp-sized pullover several miles beyond. Willi, Ad, and Kiran debated the merits of staying there for the night versus moving ahead two miles. We slept while they argued. Ten minutes later they decided to move on, apparently for no good reason. Annoyed, we packed up and returned to the noise and fumes of travel. Directly below Lata, the truck stopped for good. Willi and Marty slept on the truck, while the rest of us followed Kiran to the Lata schoolhouse to sleep.

I was discouraged. A team we were not. Several incidents in New Delhi, such as the packing, had indicated a serious lack of individual responsibility by some members and no attempt whatever by the two leaders to delegate responsibility. The trip from New Delhi to Lata had been mentally and physically exhausting for many of us because we had not stopped for proper food and rest. I felt these were decisions the team expected Ad and Willi, as leaders of the expedition, to make. We needed someone who could take thirteen diverse opinions from individuals perfectly capable of leading themselves and organize them into a single purpose.

I couldn't sleep, so I lay awake in the moonlight pondering the last few days of our trip, writing down what I felt we must discuss in a group meeting the next morning.

I approached Willi early the next day. He was still in the truck, but beginning to stir in the slanting rays of the early morning sunshine.

"Willi, let's have a group meeting."

"Fine," he said. "We'll have it as soon as everyone's up from the schoolhouse. Beautiful morning, isn't it?"

The expedition members gathered in a semicircle in front of the truck. Willi and Ad sat on the rusty iron bumper.

"I hope this meeting will unify the team," I began cautiously. "We are too loosely organized to climb a mountain like Nanda Devi the way we are now. We each need some responsibility to draw us together into a team.

"Willi, Ad," I continued even more carefully, "I feel we need only one leader. The two of you can only debate and find it difficult to reach an agreement because you don't want to oppose each other. Willi, back in the States you said we had a two-headed monster—Ad in the East and you in the West. Maybe it's time to change that. Maybe we need a single leader to make us a team."

Both Willi and Ad quickly became defensive and clearly considered my speech out of line, an insult to their authority. They weren't hearing what I was really trying to say.

"Dad, calm down," Devi chimed in. "You're looking at him like you're going to explode. He's only trying to help the expedition run a little smoother."

I couldn't believe what I had just heard. Although I had

just insinuated, in a less-than-tactful way, that we needed a different type of leadership, Devi, who I thought would stand behind her father on the issue, had clearly opened her mind to what I was trying to say.

I continued with examples. "Look at the past few months, Willi. We are still unsure of how much equipment to take, what food to bring. No one bothered to find out if Lou Reichardt is coming or whether John Evans will be able to make it. We haven't stopped for rest or food. We've been cutting corners on health by eating in crummy restaurants. What it boils down to is that I don't see anyone, especially you or Ad, making firm decisions and sticking to them."

Ad was justifiably irritated. He insisted that he organized the trip and it was done well. I couldn't argue his point, but once the team was together the organization had fallen apart.

Willi calmed down enough to explain his view. "I don't feel strong leadership is essential with a group of people as experienced as this. We're not two-year-olds who need a mother, but adults capable of making our own decisions. I don't feel that we should have to hold your hand." He recalled the 1963 Everest Expedition where he felt the leadership had been too overbearing and there had been some conflict because of it.

"I don't want my hand held, Willi," I replied, "nor do I want to see an expedition with no leadership. What I would like to see is some delegation of responsibility to each person, like seeing that our lunches are made, that latrines are built, boiled water is available, and tents pitched—things that are essential to a smooth, healthy expedition."

The rest of the group agreed with me, but with slightly more tact. Within a half hour, most of the members had agreed to take some type of job to oversee during the trek in.

Willi angrily cut loose at me a final time for the sloppy master list of equipment that had been made in Delhi. It was so bad that all the boxes would have to be reopened, their contents listed accurately, and perishables bagged in plastic to protect them from monsoon rains.

"You were there most of the time and you've been on expeditions before. Why didn't you make sure it was done right?" Willi fumed.

He was right. Having been on other expeditions, I knew better. I had failed to take a responsibility when I knew the job was being done poorly. I told him so and that I would be responsible for that job during the repacking. We broke up and almost eagerly started repacking loads, cooking breakfast, boiling water, and, in general, performing as a team.

The day went smoothly. By afternoon we had accomplished all that needed to be done in order to begin the trek early the next morning. Kiran had arranged for eighty porters to carry expedition loads and 120 goats to carry the porters' food. The *bhakrawallas*, native goat shepherds, busily filled the heavy woven goat saddlebags with about fifteen kilograms of *atta* flour. *Daal*, rice, and even our ropes were also sewn into the goat bags.

Late in the afternoon, Jim, Peter, Andy, Elliot, and I went down to the Dhaoli River and bathed in the numbing glacial water. After a game of frisbee we returned through the bright green stalks of native marijuana plants to the schoolhouse where Surrendra, our newly appointed IMF cook, had prepared a superb curried meal of potatoes, *chapatis*, and *daal*. He later served the customary hot "Sherpa tea"—equal parts of sugar, cream, and water with a dash of tea. We looked forward to the morning and the beginning of our trek deep into the Garhwal Himalayas.

THREE

We crouched under the slate awning of the schoolhouse as seething clouds hid the forests and terraced fields. Surrendra appeared through the drizzle carrying a dented aluminum bucket of steaming mush, watery from the lack of oatmeal. He was followed closely by Jatendra, stepping carefully so as not to spill the heavily sweetened Sherpa tea.

We were awake early to pack for the day's push from Lata at 6,500 feet to Lata Kharak (the high pasturage of Lata) at 12,000 feet. Our route to the Sanctuary would avoid the lower four miles of the Rishi Gorge, a vertical-walled, trailless portion of the river's path better left to the wild sheep and golden eagles of the Garhwal.

Jagatsingh,* the head porter from Lata, was busily distributing loads to each porter. He was dressed as a village head should be, in a fairly new beige sweater, clean black cotton pants, and large-lugged khaki tennis shoes. He strutted around the porters, gesturing wildly at them and at the loads that needed moving. Sharp and variable, his Hindi was punctuated with shouts or mumbles, depending on which persuaded his men to work. Each reacted according to the weight of the load, which they always maintained was over the limit. Invariably, the one with the "overweight" load would call the other porters over to compare and help argue his case. Kiran, our liaison officer, would take out his scale, weigh

*Indians from the northern regions who are not members of the Sikh religion attach *singh* to their names, as in Jagatsingh. Nirmal Singh, who is a Sikh, demonstrates the traditional Sikh use of *singh*, which attaches it as a separate name.

the load and, depending on the outcome, either take out the unnecessary weight or walk triumphantly away. Kiran followed Jagatsingh and wrote the name and wage of each porter on his paymaster's sheet as he assigned a load. Each porter would be paid fifteen rupees per day, an amount equivalent to $1.25.

The porters were a ragged bunch, dressed more like New York transients than village Indians. Some were of Tibetan origin with narrow eyes and maple brown skin. They had short legs, large bones, and thick muscles. Others were thin and small-muscled with fair skin, their curly hair light brown to deep black. We could never be sure how far up the mountain they would go.

Up until this expedition, I had had very little experience supervising porters. On Dhaulagiri in 1973 the Sherpas had dealt with them. Up the trail, the porters were like a bunch of boy scouts on a weekend outing—jovial, laughing, smoking. Most were young, some even sixteen years old. I had fun with them and took photographs. They soon experienced my hotheadedness, however, when they demanded more money or refused to carry.

Each man carried as near to sixty pounds as could be packed in each load, regardless of age. Seldom did any of them remove the layers of tattered clothing, consisting of several cotton shirts, a sweater, and a tweed or plain wool jacket. Their garments were more patches and shreds than original cloth. Buttons seemed a scarce commodity, as did fly zippers for trousers, probably more for convenience than expense. Wool pants were patched at the seat, knees, and pockets. Few porters, if any, wore underwear. Socks were like their shoes, which never seemed to fit, and were most likely hand-me-downs from fathers or uncles. Unlike Nepali porters who prefer to carry barefoot, most Garhwalis wear black rubber oxfords or, if well-off, a large-lugged Indian army "tennis" shoe that proved ideal for the muddy trails into Nanda Devi.

I was surprised to see the porters carry the heavy loads as if they were backpacks. Instead of soft foam-padded shoulder straps, they used quarter-inch manila rope or a long narrow strip of cotton. A knot called a "porter hitch," which could be pulled to release the load quickly in an emergency, was tied last under the armpit. During the trek I was to appreciate this safety measure more fully because the porters were in constant danger of deadly falls in steep terrain.

Few of them seemed to be free of illness or skin ailments. Raw sores abounded on hands and feet. All had hacking chest coughs and were constantly hawking and spitting. The American climbers were overly cautious on lending clothing or sleeping bags to them for fear the vermin that infested every stitch of their unwashed clothing would invade our equipment.

Yet in many ways the porters were more careful about their health habits than we were. They would never put their lips to a bottle or cup, as we did, but would pour the contents from a distance as if from a wine flask. They were reluctant to shake hands, unless out of embarrassment when we offered ours, because they considered this to be unclean.

I mused about the porters while I sat above the road and took pictures of the soggy scene below. Sahibs (as male Europeans and high-caste Asians in India are called), hidden beneath black umbrellas, drifted aimlessly about waiting for the first porters to struggle up the hill and lead the way.

"John," Jim called from below. "Let's get started."

We spotted a brightly dressed porter with the eighty-pound medical box and began following him up the trail.

Neither Jim nor I bothered to fill our water bottles at the stream above the road, preferring to wait for cleaner water. The syrupy fluid flowing through Lata had a disagreeable smell and feel. Chances were good that we would soon cross water farther up the trail and possibly avoid dysentery.

Marty, soaked from the misty drizzle, moved in behind us as we began the 5,500-foot climb to Lata Kharak. The porter we had chosen to lead the way turned in the village of Lata, evidently to eat his last breakfast at home for the next two weeks. The trail appeared fairly obvious, so we continued on without much trouble.

The wide rocky trail, shaded by thorn bushes that tore

at my umbrella, wound upward, then traversed along terraced barley fields, yellow-green in the early summer. After an hour's climb, we marched into a shaded, thick-foliaged streambed with a quiet brook. Jim disappeared into the undergrowth above with our water bottles, away from the droppings of the hundreds of goats that had recently passed by. Marty and I took shelter from the rain in a soot-blackened cave, ate our *chapatis*, and waited for Jim, who soon returned soaked from the wet underbrush.

Jim and I continued on, leaving Marty to visit with several sahibs who had caught up with us. We climbed out of the streambed and approached the *bhakrawallas*, who were milling under a large pine tree. The goats were unloaded and their saddlebags were stacked neatly beside the shepherds' fire. Motioning at the sky and at the goat bags, the herders began talking to us in Hindi as if we knew exactly what they were saying. They soon made it perfectly clear that this was where they intended to spend the night. It was only 9:00 A.M.

"Do you get the feeling it's raining too hard for them, Jim?" I asked.

"Kiran will get them to move," Jim replied. "Let's keep going."

The faint roar of the Dhaoli below indicated we had gained several thousand feet above the river, but the misty clouds prevented us from seeing our hard-earned reward. Soon the splatter of raindrops on the broad leaves and the squish of mud under our tennis shoes were the only sounds attesting to our silent exertion. Occasionally the mist would clear, unveiling steep forests and sharp vegetated ridges in the distance.

"John, what do you say we wait for the others?" Jim asked. "This doesn't seem like the right way to go."

It wasn't. The rain had stopped and we could see the trail petered out to a goat path beyond.

Most of the group straggled up the trail to our rest area. Ad declared a lunch stop and those carrying group food produced canned cheese, peanuts, and *chapatis*. We waited for more than an hour while Devi ran back down the trail to find the rest of the expedition. Kiran had given his word to the shepherds that it would not rain the rest of the day and had persuaded them to continue. As we had feared, the porters and remaining climbers had taken the correct trail farther back and were now some distance ahead of us, ascending a steep gully.

We caught the last of the porters at the junction of the two trails and followed Ad into the gully.

"Am I slowing you up?" Ad kept asking.

"Don't worry about it, Ad," we assured him. "This is an excellent pace."

At age sixty-two, Ad, his strong legs swelling from the labor, seemed a man of forty. Carrying a fairly light pack, he entered camp each day ahead of most of the sahibs. Ad had mentioned to Jim the previous day that he didn't feel needed and was thinking of not going in with us.

I needed to burn up some energy so I made time, climbing steadily. I passed porter after porter, some resting, others laboring up the fifty-degree trail. Soon I surmounted the ridge to a meadow of flowers and deep grass. Jim was minutes behind.

We were tired but much too thirsty to relax and followed the first porters into a clump of birch and alder just below us. A porter dug a hole in the soil until a trickle of water began to flow. With a large leaf, he made a funnel spout and we had a slow but steady supply of water that would have to satisfy the needs of over one hundred sahibs and porters.

Within a half hour other climbers appeared, exhausted and soaked. As each porter shuffled into camp, I stacked the loads they dropped at my feet. Elliot arrived last with the much-needed master list for the boxes. We quickly located the three four-man tents, dinner, and gear for the night.

While the rest of the team were setting out their own gear, Devi was showing the porters how to set up the old Bishop four-man tent Ad had brought along. She patiently connected the aluminum poles and spoke in her broken Hindi, adding Nepali when her Hindi wasn't understood. I helped her set the old, worn rain-fly away from the nylon tent with sticks to keep the rain off the porters. Devi rounded up additional foam mats from the sahibs so the porters would be comfortable sleeping on the ground.

At dinner, she added a special cheese mix to the noodles, soup, and meat that Surrendra had prepared. It was a superb meal. There seemed to be no end to Devi's energy.

Marty, Andy, Elliot, Pete, and I positioned ourselves, sardine-like, in the four-man tent. The other six sahibs occupied the second tent nearby. I was careful to get next to the door, not only to leave easily during the night, but also to avoid—as much as possible—the nauseating gas that would be produced by five sahibs eating the local food. The soft drizzle hitting the tent put us all to sleep quickly.

We were awake and packing our gear at 5:30 A.M., although we thought we probably would not move because of the night's continuous rain. Kiran returned from the shepherds' camp to inform us they would not move in the rain again.

"They insist their *atta* will spoil if it gets wetter," Kiran said, and shrugged helplessly. *Atta* was carried in the goats' saddlebags, along with *daal* and rice.

"Would they be satisfied if we gave them plastic bags for it?" Willi asked. "With the *atta* in the plastic bags inside of the wool saddlebags, they won't have another excuse for stalling."

The sahibs decided to stay put for another day while the shepherds repacked the *atta*. We hoped the rain would stop for tomorrow. Devi took out her pipe flute and Willi his harmonica and they began playing camping songs. We sang along while the shepherds packed.

We later discovered the *bhakrawallas* had tricked us with the wet *atta* complaint. Jim learned from one of the porters that only the flour next to the wool gets wet and then prevents any more moisture from entering the bag. By the time we had learned this, though, the shepherds had several hundred of our plastic bags and an extra day's pay.

The rain turned to a misty drizzle. Jim and I played with our tripod and cameras, hoping to capture the beauty of the flowers in the area. Always looking for an excuse for a celebration, the porters slaughtered a young goat, skinned it, cut it up, and then pulverized it. They fried the blood and passed it around as a treat. Many of the sahibs had a reluctant morsel.

Jim and I discussed Lou Reichardt and John Evans, both of whom had yet to join the expedition. There was no question in my mind that a new technical route was impossible without them. Reichardt and Evans were seasoned veterans, knew what to expect, knew the dangers involved, knew the work necessary to fix lines, to work to exhaustion day after day. A team without them was mediocre in strength and short on technical expertise. According to some others of the group, however, it could handle a new route just fine.

Age and differing motives were against us from the start. Not only did we have older members of unknown physical strength, we had untested, inexperienced youth. I considered Ad Carter strictly an organizer—base camp staff only. Willi was borderline because of his crippled feet and his age (although he would prove far stronger and more determined than I had at first thought). Then there was Elliot, Peter, Andy, and Devi. I didn't know much about Elliot; he didn't have much of a climbing history. Peter was off in the clouds since his too-recent breakup with Marty. Andy seemed unstable to me because of what he told me at our first meeting at the airport in New York. Devi I knew to be very inexperienced. Unfortunately, she had influence. She could convince others to eat the Indian food, to forgo the fixed lines, to do away with toilet tissue. Her ideas were far too radical for me. Marty, a strong climber, wanted the alpine-style ascent—without fixed lines. With a team this size, I was skeptical. To make matters even more complicated, heaven knows what the Indians were thinking.

Jim States was steady. He was strong, determined, and could lead technically difficult ground but was content to let me lead, if necessary, for speed and efficiency. I could count on him.

The evening's weather looked promising before dark. After some discussion on the merits of goat meat (several climbers were feeling ill), we turned in early. Marty and Andy, on the far side of the tent, seemed to be doing more tossing and turning than usual. I took a sleeping pill and went to sleep without difficulty.

The morning of July 16 was cool and clear, as promised. Nanda Ghunti (19,833 feet), covered with fresh snow, held off the incoming clouds and lesser peaks surrounded us.

Marty, Andy, and Jim were ill with severe chills, diarrhea, and vomiting. Jim had been in and out of his tent all night and evidently the tossing and turning of Marty and Andy in our tent was due to chills. Peter also was affected. Marty needed medication and chatted with Jim about her symptoms. He gave her some tetracycline, and Lomotil to check the diarrhea. As in all such illnesses, especially at high altitude, Jim recommended she take fluids continuously.

Andy, barely out of the tent before it was dropped and packed for transport, found Jim to explain his symptoms. He wanted to remain another day at Lata Kharak with Marty. Jim agreed, but the tents, stoves, and food were already packed and up the hill. Andy still wanted to talk it over with Willi.

As I sat eating my breakfast, Andy approached Willi. He asked that a tent, some food, and porters be left behind for him and Marty. Willi thought Andy was an hour too late. The gear was disappearing over the mountain with the porters as they spoke.

Looking Andy over, he asked, "What's wrong, can't you make it?"

"That's not the point, Willi," Andy replied defensively. "Rather, is it worth the risk?"

Willi prevailed. The discussion ended quietly and Andy returned to his packing. Jim agreed they could all move ahead. The year before, Jim had amoebic dysentery at 16,000 feet in Bolivia but still climbed 20,000-foot Huayna Potosi by a new route. This, added to the gear being gone, made him think that Marty, Andy, and he could make the short trek that day.

I loaded Jim's gear into my pack so he wouldn't have to carry a load, then followed him up the hill at a snail's pace. Marty was very weak but at first refused help from a porter to carry her load. After some arguing she gave in. Another porter carried Andy's pack.

The healthy sahibs picked a sick person to stay with and help during the day's march. Jim and I followed the porters to the crest of a flagstone ridge, then traversed along a barely visible goat path. With the porters far ahead of our slow pace and the other sahibs some way behind, Jim casually meandered along, stopping frequently to swallow Lomotil and fluids for his constant diarrhea. I followed, enjoying the whimsical walk, and supplied Jim with water, toilet tissue, and a few laughs at his expense.

Before long we climbed abruptly to Dharansi Pass, pockmarked with rock cairns, and traversed along rock ribs, slowly gaining more height. Clouds rose from the valley, cutting loose periodic rain squalls that chilled us at 14,000 feet. Ad and Elliot, with a group of porters, caught us below a rocky gully, said a brief hello, and disappeared into the swirling mist. An occasional voice drifted down to us, ghostlike. They soon were gone completely. At the end of the gully and a long traverse we arrived at a wide meadow to camp.

Jim relaxed while Nirmal, Kiran, and I pitched one tent and helped Ad and Elliot throw up the other. Surrendra was already busy boiling water and cooking the evening meal, so I descended to a small hummock to dig a respectable latrine, knowing full well how often it would be used by those who were ill.

The others arrived two hours later in groups of twos and threes. Marty was a mess. Each of her arms was slung over the neck of a porter. She was semicomatose: they literally dragged her into camp.

Devi, who had been mothering Marty all day, arrived just ahead of her to prepare her own sleeping bag for Marty. Marty was placed inside of the bag and Devi crawled in to help control her violent shivering.

Marty hadn't been able to drink, nor would she continue to take the drugs Jim had given her during the trek from Lata Kharak. She worsened at every rise, dropping down to sit, saying, "I can't go any farther."

The others were able to get her to camp only by persuasion and finally by carrying her.

Jim checked Marty as she came into camp and after dinner and several times during the rainy night, but could do little in the way of a proper exam. Devi stayed with Marty all night.

Early the next morning, on July 17, those of us who were well had a short meeting and decided to wait until noon before moving camp and Marty. Jim felt she needed fluids first before being moved. A half hour later Jim approached me after examining Marty.

"John," he said, "Marty looks pretty bad. Take a look at her eyes when you get a chance."

At the "sick" tent, Marty was struggling to stand up and make it outside the tent with Devi's help. I knew Marty was in trouble the instant I saw her eyes. They were opaque, dull, roaming. She tried to speak coherently but her tongue seemed heavy and useless and her dry lips moved in slow motion. She wasn't aware of her surroundings. I felt we couldn't move her down the mountain quickly enough. It was still raining cold and hard.

Jim had said earlier that morning that her symptoms were dysentery, fluid and electrolyte depletion, hypothermia, and nausea. He felt that the most important thing to do now was to persuade her to take fluids. After the morning checkup, he realized that there was no way to put fluids into her because of the constant vomiting and diarrhea. His irritation grew as he remembered he had been pressured into leaving intravenous fluids behind.

I left the "sick" tent and headed straight for Willi, walking up to camp from the latrine.

"Willi, we've got to move Marty out of here now to a lower elevation," I burst out.

He began to argue but I broke in and told him what I had just seen. I seemed to convince him of her immediate danger and he and I went back to the tent to arrange her evacuation. Nirmal picked three strong porters to help carry Marty, and the group decided to evacuate her to Dibrugheta, two thousand feet lower and the next stage ahead.

Willi, an expert on knots and rope handling, improvised a seat harness out of a climbing rope in which to carry Marty piggyback. Devi dressed her in rainproof clothing. Unable to stand by herself, Marty was lifted onto Nirmal's back. Willi, the three porters, and I surrounded Nirmal to help him keep his balance in the slick mud. The rest of the climbers would pick up camp and follow us to Dibrugheta as soon as possible.

We traversed out of the bowl of the meadow to a 14,000-foot pass, decorated at the crest by a porter-built rock archway. The terrain was treacherous even for those of us with normal loads. Dharamsingh carried Marty next, dancing cautiously from slick rock to slimy mud with the skill of a man who has lived all his life in the Garhwal.

We continued across another wide-open meadow, taking frequent stops for porter changes and to let Marty rest. At each stop she apologized in her delirium for being so much trouble.

"I'm sorry, please let me walk," she would drawl. "I don't want to be any trouble."

"Marty, this is no trouble at all, just relax and tell us when you feel sick or want to stop," I would say, turning away to hide my tears.

Elliot and several porters passed us, hurrying for camp so it would be ready when we arrived. Marty worsened.

"John, catch the porter with the medical box and have him stick close by," Willi whispered.

I removed my pack in order to move more quickly down the dangerous slope in pursuit of the porter.

"Elliot! Elliot!" I yelled, desperate. "Stop the medical box!"

I ran back up to the rim of the gorge in time to help the porters who were now dragging Marty down the loose, precipitous slope.

"How are you feeling, Marty?" I spoke slowly so she could understand.

"Oh, John . . ." She answered with a thick tongue. "I'm so tired. Please forgive me."

"Take some water, Marty," Willi told her. "You've got to get some down."

She tried but immediately vomited.

"We've got to go now, Marty, are you ready?" Willi asked.

"I don't feel good," she replied. "Could we stay longer?"

Up to that point, Marty wouldn't give up the ski poles she used for hiking, but we insisted she forget them and concentrate on holding her arms around the two porters. She was now 130 pounds of putty. Moving quickly, the soaked porters seemed to know that getting her down would save her life. We couldn't have done it alone. Descending the mud and rock took two porters on either side of her. I descended backward before her, placing her feet so she could support herself a little.

The rain diminished, but the terrain became worse. At the bottom we crossed the creek bed. We paused briefly to wash the mud from our legs and clothes while Marty rested. Jim caught up with us and checked Marty. He continued on ahead to set up the medical tent.

It took all six of us to haul Marty up a rock step above the stream and through a flowered meadow to enter Dibrugheta, a heavily forested glade next to a running brook.

Marty was taken into a prepared tent, stripped of her wet clothes, and placed in a thick down sleeping bag. Jim began examining her. He gave her medication for nausea and a suppository in hopes of stopping the vomiting. There were no quick remedies. He was afraid we were going to lose her.

It was still early in the afternoon. Willi and Jim stayed with Marty constantly as we finally realized the seriousness of her illness. Jim began an accurate record of fluid intake and output. Half a cup of Tang was forced every fifteen minutes for salt and fluids.

Around 6:00 P.M., just as things began to look their bleakest, Lou Reichardt arrived in camp. In one day, he and his porter had climbed two-and-a-half stages from Lata Kharak below. Lou was indefatigable, a scientist in a strong athlete's body. I hadn't seen him in two years, but I knew from the look in his eyes and his firm handshake that he was as determined as I to get to Nanda

Devi. I knew we had a chance at a new route now. Lou greeted everyone warmly.

We filled Lou in on Marty's condition with relief. As a biophysicist at Harvard Medical School, Lou was actively involved in brain research. Any decisions concerning Marty were now in good hands. Lou's area of expertise was the brain, and Marty was definitely having problems with hers.

A short group meeting was held at 6:30 P.M. Jim outlined Marty's problems and what he thought was the best course to take medically. Pairs of climbers were chosen to take two-hour shifts through the night with Marty. Willi and Jim took the first shift, while Kiran and I were to take the second. Jim ended the meeting, but seemed aware of my awkward silence.

"John, you seem to have something to say that you're holding in. What is it?"

"I think Marty's condition is serious and she should be evacuated."

"Does anyone else have anything to offer?" Jim asked.

No one offered an opinion.

Devi worked feverishly around camp that afternoon and later cooked a cheese sauce for our potatoes, which became our favorite meal. I had been listening to her contribute good judgment and compassion to the group discussions. Although she was young and idealistic, she would defer to experience. She was eager to learn. I was amazed at her energy and willingness to help others, especially Marty. My impressions of her as stubborn and single-minded were certainly changing, although I still had the feeling that Devi considered me a male chauvinist.

Andy and Peter sacked out when they entered camp. They were just beginning to get over their illnesses and needed rest. Lou, Kiran, Nirmal, and I talked for a brief spell in our tent.

I couldn't sleep. My discussion with Lou that evening had been about the symptoms of cerebral edema, an accumulation of fluid in the brain cavity. I went over each symptom carefully in my mind and correlated these to Marty's problems, which I was so familiar with by then. Without a word to Lou, I slipped from the tent and stumbled over in the dark to Marty's tent, where Jim and Willi kept watch.

Opening the tent flap, I whispered, "I think she has some symptoms of cerebral edema and we should put her on oxygen."

Surprised, Jim and Willi looked at each other.

"We were discussing that very thing," Jim said.

I woke Elliot for the master list and he and I searched for the masks and regulators that fit the oxygen bottles.

Willi set up the Horbein oxygen system on Marty and gave her a full flow, five liters per minute. Whether it was the medication, time, oxygen, or sheer will, Marty became alert and began retaining fluids almost instantly. After three hours of oxygen she was alert and coherent. We let her sleep for some time, occasionally helping her to urinate and drink Tang. By 4:30 A.M. she took Lomotil and a cup of Tang by herself and was reasonably rational.

Jim gave her a complete exam early on the morning of July 18 and found her problems less extensive. At a 7:00 A.M. meeting Jim suggested Marty be evacuated, but he would give us his final recommendation at noon.

"We'll let Jim handle it," Willi said. "He knows what he is doing and when he brings back an answer, that's it."

We agreed. Jim needed time to evaluate the circumstances and the implications of his decision. Jim, Lou, and I retired to the stream for an hour to bathe and unwind. Lou said he felt Marty had definite neurological problems—amnesia, spasticity, inability to articulate or control her eye movements—and should have further tests before going higher up the mountain.

We returned to camp to find Devi leading Marty down to the stream for a wash. Everyone but Jim was excited. Several of the members came over and happily expressed what a remarkable recovery she'd made. The majority of the team now thought that at the next meeting Jim would certainly say Marty could continue.

"She doesn't need that right now," Jim whispered to me.

I was impressed Marty was even standing after the previous night.

Jim asked me to write down his thoughts about Marty's problems while he debated his choices.

"We could have two extremes," he began. "First, Marty could recover fully, catch the team and become a productive member and all one hundred people on this expedition could make it to Base safely without a physician.

"Second," he continued, "she could die or a lack of a physician could endanger the lives of the other one hundred individuals who must continue on.

"What we have here," Jim said, "is a person who was in a life-threatening situation. She had a cerebral condition for which the diagnosis wasn't clear. Medically I'm not prepared to deal with additional confirmatory diagnosis."

He gave an example. "If a football player was knocked out on the field, the coach wouldn't send him back in without further tests, such as a brain scan or EEG to find out if additional damage had occurred that could not be seen. This is the situation we're faced with. Essentially, I've got only borderline data that points to a real problem, and on top of that, I don't know what's happened to her brain."

Jim had to consider not only Marty's welfare, but also the team's. What would her evacuation or recovery time mean to the team? We all liked Marty. In fact, Peter—and possibly Andy—were infatuated, perhaps in love, with her. Peter wanted the whole team to wait two weeks until she might recover. At one point or another, Peter, Andy, and Elliot talked about escorting her out. If they left it was possible that only Andy would return. The entire expedition was at stake.

We also had to worry about the food supply of the porters. We had eight days' supply left for them, giving us five days to reach Base, and three days' supply for the porters to use on their return trip. Any more unscheduled rain or sick days and we would have to wait for the porters to return to Lata for more food to pack us the rest of the way in.

Just after Marty returned to her tent the noon meeting

started. Jim gave a complete diagnosis of Marty's condition and the possibilities of recovery or further damage.

"I feel that with these findings, Marty should be evacuated as soon as possible," he concluded.

There was a long silence while the full weight of Jim's decision sank in. This was not what most of the members had expected.

"I think we should lift this responsibility from Jim's shoulders," Willi suggested. "As a doctor he is bound to consider the worst possible results and not necessarily the most likely ones. Nothing can be sure from the diagnosis and we're all here to take our chances."

Jim was obviously shocked. Only that morning the group had voiced its complete support of any medical decision he should make.

"You have to understand, I want her to stay as much as any of you," Jim added. "There could be serious complications with the head or clotting. We can't determine this without further tests."

Peter argued that the decision of sending Marty out could hurt her more emotionally. Lou and I dismissed this.

Everyone sought an alternative. Willi was pushing to let Marty stay put, recuperate, and join the team farther up the mountain. That sounded like apple pie and ice cream to Andy, Peter, Devi, and Elliot. But Marty needed tests on her brain, rest, good food, and a lower altitude. To wait could mean permanent damage.

Willi challenged Lou's feeling that losing part of the brain was more serious than other bodily injury. Although Willi admitted losing a good part of his mental acuity on Mt. Everest in 1963, he didn't think that the richness of his life was reduced.

Andy, who had said earlier he respected a physician's decision and that we should abide by it, was completely silent.

Ad felt Marty should be evacuated, since that was the doctor's opinion, but refused to take this stand during the meeting. He kept asking for Lou's "expert testimony." Lou said again and again she should be evacuated.

I supported Jim's decision intensely, believing Marty to be in serious condition.

Kiran, somewhat off the point, reiterated his disappointing experience in 1974 on Changabang, when he had injured his shoulder. He was not allowed by the other members to make a summit attempt because they were worried he could not hold his own and would lessen the chances of everyone's success.

"The decision boils down to this," Willi continued. "Do we have the right to make a judgment medically when we're not sure of the implications to Marty? Jim is guessing on the projected outcome."

Willi's opinion of doctors and their diagnoses was more than clear. After serving as director of Peace Corps doctors in Nepal for several years, Willi felt that a doctor's role should be limited. The meeting had become a battle of philosophies.

"We have to go by the past forty-eight hours," Jim insisted. "Marty shouldn't be exposed to further trauma. She was semicomatose for forty hours, delirious, and had severe neurologic problems. Can we ignore these symptoms just because she's beginning to feel better? As the physician here, I'm responsible." Jim knew that any decision was going to reflect on his medical judgment. If he let Marty continue and she died of complications, such as a clot to the brain or cerebral edema, he would be condemned by both the mountaineering and the medical communities. He had chosen the only course open to him as a professional.

"Let's find out Marty's views on this," Willi volunteered. "I would like to talk with her alone if everyone agrees."

I didn't like the idea. Willi could be very persuasive. "I think someone else should talk to her," I told the group. I wasn't wishy-washy and wasn't about to see Willi give the team that grandfatherly reassurance as if he alone had the answers. He was the "mountain man" to a lot of people, a guru of sorts—and a master of persuasion. There was a time and place for his philosophies. I wasn't going to see Marty hurt.

"Willi, you can be too damn persuasive, even to the point of talking her into staying," I said.

"That's not my reason for talking to her, John," cooed Willi. "I only want her to voice her opinion in this problem, since it affects her more than anyone else. I won't try to persuade Marty one way or another."

I reluctantly accepted his proposal. The meeting broke up and everyone relaxed a little. We agreed to meet again at 3:00 P.M. to continue the discussion.

Kiran and Nirmal were in our tent resting when I entered.

"Nirmal and I agree with you on evacuating Marty," Kiran told me. "Nirmal thinks she should be taken out immediately, not just for her good, but for the group's."

"Damn it, Kiran, then say it to the entire group," I demanded. "Jim needs vocal support on this decision, not hearsay."

During the lull before the next meeting I visited with Marty.

"You're looking much better, Marty," I said. "I thought for a while we were going to lose you."

"Tell me, John," she said. "Do you think I should go out? Was I that ill?"

"Marty, in my opinion, you were as good as dead. You're lucky to be alive."

I left to walk around in the forest, wondering what all the arguments would do to the morale of the expedition. Jim and I decided not to talk with each other between the meetings. It was obvious some of the members didn't like my strong stand in support of Jim and felt I was influencing his decision. How could I back Jim and not be accused of manipulating him? And why was I being singled out in the "power struggle" when Jim was the doctor and had taken the responsibility on himself to send her out? I wanted Marty to continue too. Why couldn't the team see that?

The afternoon meeting was held in another tent in the far corner of the camp. We filed in and sat against the tent walls.

Willi began. "I explained to Marty our last meeting and Jim's decision . . . This is her decision: her first choice is to recover here for several days, proceed to Base Camp, and climb above. But if any team member seriously objects to this, she will return to the U.S.''

Jim again reminded the group of the medical implications and diagnosis. At his last check, she still had slurred speech, dizziness, decreased visual acuity, and problems with balance. He stood firm on his decision.

''Willi,'' I persisted, ''part of the reason Marty didn't recover like the other three is because she wouldn't eat the food or drink the water to keep up her strength. She refused to take medication. If she goes on to Base, the same thing is sure to happen.''

''We'll get Marty to promise to eat right,'' Willi said. ''That's really no problem.''

Andy felt that Marty had the right as patient to refuse Jim's advice, arguing that the doctor can only suggest, not command. Certainly no one would disagree had we been at sea level. Willi sided with Andy: the group could not deprive Marty of her right to accept or reject a professional opinion. Devi agreed with Andy.

Marty, obviously weak, appeared in the doorway of the tent as Andy spoke. No one said a word.

''I want to listen,'' she insisted, still slurring her words. ''I don't want any more arguing. If there's any trouble because of me, I want to go back.''

Someone assured her that we weren't arguing.

With Marty in earshot, Willi played his last hand.

''She has said she will return to the States if anybody objects,'' he started. He looked at me. ''Do you object?''

''Yes,'' I replied, knowing I was on the spot. ''I don't want Marty on a rope with me when her problem may return at high altitude.'' The excuse sounded feeble.

Turning to Marty I said, ''I don't feel you're able to make a proper decision on this issue.''

Willi was irate. Devi broke in, trying to calm her father down.

''I've had enough!'' Jim suddenly burst out in tears.

He leaned over to Marty and gave her a hug, sobbing, ''I only want to save your life and do what is best for you!'' Jim spun to face the group. ''We are dealing with a life and death issue. When you want to talk about life and death in a realistic sense," he demanded, "come and get me."

He broke away from the tent and stormed into the forest. Marty left also, very upset. Peter followed.

The air was so taut I thought it would snap. Willi was angry and turned to me instantly, glaring.

"There seems to be a power struggle here," he snapped.

"I don't want anything to do with it, Willi," I said calmly. "I'm only backing Jim on the medical issue."

Peter entered the tent. "Marty has decided not to go on," he said quietly. We separated with Pete's words.

"I thought she should go out," Ad whispered to me as we left the tent.

It irritated me that he hadn't said one word to that effect during the entire argument. If he, as coleader, had asserted his opinion earlier it might have been a less emotional debate.

The cool air and smell of wood and ferns bolstered my spirits. I found Jim by the brook and we walked briskly up to the flowered meadow. We talked about the meeting and tried to find the reasons why it had gotten out of hand.

"I'm going to ask for a helicopter," Jim concluded. "Ad said he will support that, but I'm afraid Willi won't."

We returned to camp for a late supper. After writing several letters, I dropped off to sleep, exhausted.

July 19 looked even worse than it sounded from inside my tent. It was 5:30 A.M. and raining buckets. Smoke drifted lazily between the giant trees. The porters sat cooking their morning rice and *chapatis*, obviously miserable in the downpour. Jatendra shoved several scalding cups of Sherpa tea through the tent door as I brought out my pen and diary. Kiran and Nirmal, still deep in their bags, were talking quietly to each other in Hindi beside me and Lou was just beginning to move.

I had the feeling we had to do something decisive this day. If we stayed another day, an argument was sure to begin again and the decision to evacuate Marty could be changed. As it was, Andy and Peter had decided to stay with Marty, along with Jim and Ad.

Lou wrote to his wife about Marty. "I am afraid Peter will go out and come in late, if at all. I don't blame him a bit, since I would make the same choice with you, but it is just the situation we warned against when we considered whether Marty should come at all. It was clear Peter's loyalty would be stronger to her than to the group . . ."

My pack was set to go, but I sensed something else was going to happen in camp—and I wanted to be there. So I delayed my departure by beginning a letter to my wife. The porters collected their loads, glancing around apprehensively as though one of us were going to accuse them of stealing. They retreated to their fires to eat and wait for our word to start for the next camp, Deodi.

Willi entered my tent and struck up a conversation about hunting. He knew some fascinating tales of man-eating tigers that originated in the Garhwal. I felt good that Willi was trying to smooth over any ill feelings.

A meeting of Ad, Lou, and Jim over the helicopter erupted into another argument with Willi. They spent several hours drafting a letter to the Indian army commandant in Joshimath requesting a helicopter. Ad decided to make it a "command decision," but hadn't consulted Willi, who was furious. Willi felt at first that Jim wanted the helicopter for show, to support his decision that Marty should be evacuated. Meanwhile, Peter, who never really believed Marty would have to do anything more drastic than spend a week recuperating, came into the tent very upset.

Marty deserved credit for defusing the situation. She said she didn't care how she went out, but wanted to go quickly.

I managed to stay out of this disagreement.

Lou found it hard to believe that "responsible Himalayan veterans" would try to destroy the physician's authority on a serious expedition.

Jim explained to Willi that moving Marty by foot over two passes of 14,000 feet in not less than two days could damage her further.

"She needs a quick, effortless evacuation," he said. "I checked her this morning and she was having trouble with her speech and coordination. Her sensory exam showed she had a decreased sense of feeling over the lower left leg and also she has no sensation on the forehead, which suggests intracranial lesions in several areas."

Willi, with this diagnosis, understood the gravity of the situation. He agreed to the helicopter evacuation. For the first time, everyone held the same opinion.

Willi confided in us that Peter had said to him that he would probably return to the U.S. with Marty.

"Let's everyone try and convince Peter that we need him and want him with us," Willi finished.

A drizzle was all that remained of the downpour that morning, so I told Jagatsingh to start the porters to the next camp. As the sahibs packed, they would follow.

I walked over to Marty's tent and knelt. She saw it was me and looked away.

"Marty, I'm not sorry for this because I want you alive. I want you healthy and not damaged permanently . . ." I strained to hear some sort of reply, but she continued to look away.

"Good-bye, Marty," I said. I left when I felt the tears start to well up. Marty didn't say anything.

I found Peter and asked him to walk up the hill with me.

"Peter," I began, "Willi told us you were thinking of going out with Marty and he wanted us to convince you to stay . . . I'm not going to do that. If you're not one hundred percent committed to the climb, it would be worse for you to continue on."

"Thanks John," he said, "for being straightforward with me. I'll have to do some more thinking."

Jim came over as I shouldered my pack.

"I'll see you in a few days, John. I guess Andy, Peter, and Ad will be with me here for a few days. We sent Dharamsingh out for the chopper this morning and he should be out tomorrow. Then all we need is good flying weather."

"Take care, Jim."

We grasped each other's arms for a moment. We had

become very close in the past few days. Afraid my emotions would surface again, I broke away quickly.

With the help of several porters, I found the obscure trail, barely visible through the dense vegetation. A final wave of good-bye and Dibrugheta, a place I longed to forget, disappeared.

The incident at Dibrugheta could have destroyed the expedition. If we were ever to climb Nanda Devi, we needed to put hurt feelings aside. But the team never was the same during the expedition or upon returning home. Willi, Andy, Devi, Peter, and Elliot would form a "second team" as we ascended the mountain: Jim States, Lou Reichardt, and I would become known as the "first team."

FOUR

The trail rose steeply from Dibrugheta through giant firs shrouded in low clouds. Porters smoked hand-rolled cigarettes and waited under the canopy of branches for the first sahibs to appear. They quietly began following me as I passed in the steady rain. With every step, I felt the tensions of Dibrugheta dissolve.

A thousand feet above Dibrugheta the muddy trail surmounted a right-angled ridge that fell away from me several thousand feet to the Rishi Ganga, barely visible in the ghostly mists below. Sunshine lit up the wet rock and brilliant vegetation on the far side of the gorge. The trail reached a crest of boulders and began seesawing through the many rock ribs that cut the exposed cliffside. Where the route seemed to disappear, porters had constructed makeshift walkways from rocks and tree branches. I stopped to wash and drink at the first stream—a small brook in a large gully strewn with boulders.

Explosions broke the quiet of the early morning. The sounds were unmistakable . . . Rockfall! I glanced up quickly to see boulders the size of Volkswagens headed straight down the gully, smashing bushes as they came. There was no time to run for the side of the gully. I dove for the only shelter, a hole underneath a table-sized rock.

I clawed, pushed, and squirmed into the small hole as each rock bounced by, sometimes only several feet away, and careened down its devastating path. My heart stopped beating, it seemed, as I waited for the end of the avalanche. As the last sound died away from below, I crawled out from under my apparently useless protection.

Without a second look, I ran for the trail and out of the gully.

Several porters rounded the ridge opposite me. They crossed the gully running slowly without stopping. One pointed out the fresh rock scars to his buddies. They slowed and passed me with the usual greeting of "Namaste, Sahib," and disappeared over the rise. For the first time I fully appreciated what the porters faced for a mere fifteen rupees a day.

Still shaking, I followed the porters in and out, up and down, along the narrow trail. The rubbery feeling in my legs slowly disappeared. Deodi, our next campsite, was several miles upstream in a heavily forested area. The walk was pleasant and I soon descended through thick forest and undergrowth to the river's edge. A hundred yards away, a poorly constructed plank bridge crossed the Rishi at a narrow bottleneck.

The Rishi Ganga, pinched by the gorge, roared into audible rage, quickening and boiling, a muddy torrent that would continue to the Dhaoli River several miles downstream.

Deodi's flat campsites, nestled among birch and rhododendron, soon bustled with activity as the porters entered camp in twos and threes, stacked their loads on the teetering pile, and hurried up the hill to find a good cave for the night. There were no "preowned" spots. It was strictly first-come, first-served.

The herders arrived with the *atta*-laden goats that hesitantly crossed the bridge and turned downriver to browse in the lush undergrowth along the river's edge. I wondered how the other sahibs were doing on the wet trail, now complicated by the droppings of 120 goats. I always made it a point to be ahead of the messy animals during the trek in. But the climbers appeared in high spirits, laughing and talking while enjoying the day's easy hike.

Jim, Andy, Peter, and Ad had stayed with Marty at Dibrugheta and would join us as soon as possible, although Peter still entertained thoughts of flying out with Marty. Andy was almost certain to join us and Jim couldn't be held back much longer.

Camp consisted of two four-man tents and a cooking tarp around which we all congregated. Many of the porters needed medical attention, or so they felt. I volunteered to take Jim's place to at least hand out pills. Several porters had horribly infected blisters from wearing the ill-fitting rubber oxfords without socks. These open wounds needed Jim's expertise, but as far as the porters were concerned, I filled in just fine.

Kiran, Nirmal, Lou, and I occupied a tent. We all liked our Indian companions. They had proven themselves to be hard workers, intelligent, and fair. Kiran impressed me as being one of the most patient men I had ever met. He insisted on teaching us the difference between Hindi and Nirmal's tongue, Punjabi.

"In Hindi the words are spoken softly, with love," Kiran instructed. "But Punjabi is a coarse, rough dialect, spoken quickly as if every word were an order like . . . NAMASTE!"

I picked up Punjabi instantly, and Nirmal broke into laughter.

"Punjabi's my style of talking," I joked. "My wife always said I never could speak softly."

The next morning we were awake and packed at 6:00 A.M. Lou and I started into a heavy fog, climbing through tall, scraggly rhododendrons for thirteen hundred vertical feet before breaking out of the undergrowth and starting to traverse the steep hillside. The sun began to melt the haze as we passed through a moss-laden forest. It was a scene from a storybook.

Our path descended sharply to the Trisuli Ganga, the only major river crossing we would face during the trek in. Although it was only 10:00 A.M., the porters had already built a solid fifteen-foot-long bridge of branches and sod across a narrow section. They built it more for the goats than for us, Kiran said, but we needed it more.

Most of the porters had crossed the river and were continuing ahead, climbing the steep bank and disappearing into the trees. I hurried across and a short distance upstream to take pictures of Elliot and Devi crossing the milky torrent.

Elliot was an enigma to me. Tall and thin, he didn't

look much like a climber. But Ad Carter had recommended him because he had climbed well in South America the previous summer. Elliot had worked hard in New Delhi. He took a back seat in the arguments because he didn't have much experience. I liked him for his easygoing manner. He had gone to Nepal with Devi before the expedition and met the group in New Delhi.

Devi fit the scene perfectly in pigtails, a paisley blouse, white Indian pajama bottoms, and thongs. No wonder she was the favorite of the porters, who called her *Didi* or "older sister." They called the rest of us merely "Sahib."

Sunny skies and clean water from a side stream called for an early lunch stop. Kiran, Nirmal, and I ate quickly, preferring to continue to Romani, the next campsite at the beginning of the Rishi Gorge. The porters had protested loudly to Kiran about the awkward long boxes we had brought to serve as load containers for them to carry, so we expected two sahibs—probably Lou and I—would have to carry several of the boxes through the gorge to show the porters it was possible and safe. I wanted to get an early afternoon start if that were the case.

Now that we were so close, I was very apprehensive about the Rishi Gorge. The impressive pictures I remembered of Tilman and Odell's 1936 expedition led me to believe there would be much technical climbing involved in the gorge. It was the crux to climbing Nanda Devi as far as I knew. How would eighty porters scale the near-vertical walls? Why hadn't I asked Ad more about the route when I was with him?

Nanda Devi has a long history of attempts to scale her main summit. The first serious breakthrough in such attempts came in 1934, when Eric Shipton and H. W. Tilman, both English mountaineers, explored the difficult but relatively safe route into the Sanctuary via the Rishi Gorge. The following autumn they found an alternative route to the beginning of the gorge.

In the summer of 1936, Tilman returned with seven other English and American climbers, including Ad Carter, and six Sherpas. After trouble with porters and sick team members, Tilman and another Englishman on the team, Noel Odell, reached the main summit of Nanda Devi on August 29. This achievement stood as the record for the highest peak then climbed until fourteen years later, when the summit of Annapurna was reached.

In 1939 a Polish team succeeded in reaching the summit of East Nanda Devi (24,391 feet), Nanda Devi's connecting sister. The feat was repeated in 1951 by the Frenchman Dubost and Sherpa Tenzing Bhotia, better known as Tenzing Norgay, who, years later, reached the summit of Everest with Sir Edmund Hillary. The French team had attempted to traverse between East Nanda Devi and the main peak, but was forced to abandon the attempt when two of its members disappeared below the main summit.

In the 1960s, rumors of a CIA-backed expedition to the summit of Nanda Devi were easy to prove. To achieve the objective of placing secret instrumentation on several peaks, climbers were helicoptered in to lower camps. Later climbers found hundreds of empty beer cans strewn around the CIA campsite and into the many small gullies nearby. The American climbers in the clandestine operation are well known in the climbing community. One of them made the first American ascent of Nanda Devi by the original route of 1936. Only recently has news been released by the CIA that several such expeditions took place.

The second official ascent of the main summit was accomplished in 1964 by an Indian team led by "Bull" Kumar, Kiran's brother. After two earlier failed attempts, in 1957 and 1961, the successful Indian team reached the summit by the route of the 1936 ascent.

In 1975 the French again tried to traverse from the east peak to the main one, but failed. Four members of that team reached the main summit by the regular route. Three other members reached the summit of East Nanda Devi, but weather forced them to retreat before attempting the traverse.

A month before our team entered the Sanctuary, the much-sought-after traverse from East Nanda Devi to the summit of the main peak was accomplished by two

Japanese climbers, Yoshinori Hashegawa and Masafumi Teramoto.

The difficulties of previous ascents of the South Face led our team to believe we would have a slim chance of success on the north side, yet we were determined to make a strong attempt to pioneer a second continuous route. We had no idea what the lower four thousand feet of our route would be like because we had no pictures of this section, and the route we had chosen for the upper eight thousand feet was obviously difficult from the pictures we did have. A tremendous task awaited us.

Romani, known as "the camp under the cliffs," was located in a narrow gorge fifty yards wide with vertical walls thousands of feet high on either side. The Rishi Ganga poured from a small V-shaped notch several hundred yards away, swept in a thundering swell past camp, and disappeared into gigantic cliffs. Large boulders dictated where we camped, and each spot was barely large enough for one tent, except for a deep cave where a flat dirt area had been cleared by previous parties. The cave walls, black from countless sooty fires, bore graffiti—mementos from several stranded European teams who were bored to the point of defacing the rock in bad weather or porter strikes.

Lou and I didn't have to carry into the gorge with the loads after all, because Kiran parleyed successfully with Jagatsingh about the problem with the boxes. But we were still too antsy to sit. Packing some rope and hardware, we started into the gorge. Picking our way two thousand feet through birch into a gully, then up a grassy slope, we topped out on a rib crest cutting the gorge. Walls rose on either side of us. We traversed easily for a quarter of a mile before coming upon two of our *bhakrawallas* tossing rocks off a steep buttress. An old, discolored manila line hung from the buttress. Our route was obvious.

The goat herders wanted to take the goats to Base Camp in order to get as much pay as possible. They were clearing the route of loose rock so the goats wouldn't kick it on one another. The goats were skilled climbers. When herded to greener pastures, they would bound up the trail. Some made remarkable leaps up small vertical rock steps, often using their neighbor's back as an intermediate step. Even so, I was still skeptical they could make it to Base Camp.

Climbing in places, walking in others, Lou and I had gone several miles when we stashed the rope and hardware for use later and returned to camp. Our getting through the gorge depended entirely on the weather. If it rained, the Rishi Gorge would be impassable. The weather looked marginal.

The goat herders decided to return to Lata after a discussion with Kiran and Willi about money. Kiran had been paying them only for the weight the goats were carrying, deducting the weight of the porter food that was eaten each day. The goat herders didn't like that deduction and decided to return. The porters, however, were delighted: extra loads meant more pay for them. They agreed to carry a double stage through the gorge and put the expedition into the Sanctuary in one day—exactly what we needed during this spell of fine weather.

As the shadows deepened into the gorge, Jim, Andy, and Peter walked into camp, having come from Dibrugheta that morning. We were all glad to see them, and in such good spirits. No matter the past differences, the anger, and the harsh words. The comradery was still there, reducing the loneliness and fear. Our relationships were tentative and fleeting; only during the expedition would we crave one another's company. Once back into the world, these relationships would trail off, to revive only on other climbs.

Jim filled us in on Marty's condition, which hadn't improved much. Her neurological symptoms were becoming more evident. On the nineteenth she had headaches and poor memory. Later she had lost sensation in her forehead and left leg, which suggested nerve damage. Marty finally knew something was wrong, Jim said, and sensed the need to get medical attention. Even Peter admitted that he now felt sending her out was the right decision.

"It was the best thing," Peter agreed. "It was just so hard to realize she wouldn't be with us."

"It was hard for all of us, Peter," I added.

That evening I found Jim relaxing next to the river, listening to the resounding echoes of the turbulent water. Now Jim was concerned about Devi. At Dibrugheta she had asked him to examine a large hernia in her inguinal area the size of two golf balls that she had developed during the packing session in New Delhi. Jim told me the hernia was reduceable—in other words, it could go back in by itself. He instructed Devi not to carry a load, but to wear the pack waist strap as a kind of truss. Jim didn't think she should have been there, but remembering the strenuous emotional battle of trying to get Marty to leave because of a life-threatening situation, he knew that Willi wouldn't agree. Little could we then anticipate the consequences of our reluctance to face Willi again on another medical issue.

We continued our candid conversation. The bond that Jim and I shared on difficult first ascents in the United States and South America was still strong.

"You saved Marty's life," I said. "Marty will realize that in time."

"But it still hurts to have mistrust among the team. How can we form into a climbing team with the kind of hostility that erupted at Dibrugheta?"

"We probably won't, Jim . . . We may have to climb this peak without them."

It was finally out in the open.

Jim and I could both see a rift in the group so wide that the chances of all of us cooperating to reach a common goal were slim. We would have to drive each other. If Jim and I could do that, we would reach the summit.

After a medical clinic that lasted long into the night, we finally drifted into sleep.

The camp was up before dawn, packing for the long double-stage trek that would take us to Pathal Khan, our next camp and inside the Sanctuary. Jim, Lou, and I began the trek, carrying more fixed line for the worst sections yet to be found.

The weather was perfect. I felt extremely fit and broke the rib crest some distance ahead of the others. I was not prepared for the view before me. Dominating the entire skyline was the gigantic form of Nanda Devi's North Face. Here was what we had come so far to attempt.

The V-notch and vertical walls of the Rishi Gorge framed the mountain's broad northern base, but she left these 16,000-foot buttresses and ridges of the Sanctuary wall and reached up another 10,000 feet into the cold, thin air.

I looked back and forth as I searched for some way up from the point we could see—around the 17,000-foot level—to the top. I imagined a line up the icy slopes, through the many rock bands intersecting the rising knife-bladed North Ridge near an ominous vertical buttress. The Buttress was clearly the crux of the climb, if we got that far.

There were some problems we would have to accept. The Buttress was between 22,000 and 24,000 feet, difficult climbing at that extreme altitude. The bands of rock sloped down toward the north, leaving us with down-sloping holds on the entire Buttress. Our work would be cut out for us.

I knew we had one strong plus in our favor. The Buttress was excellent climbing rock—solid metamorphic quartzite. Although quartzite often lacks continuing crack systems and good holds because of its glasslike fracturing, the climbing would most likely be safe. From the top of the Buttress the route seemed straightforward, with only one difficult-looking rock step barring our way to the summit.

The difficulties of previous ascents of the South Face led our team to believe we would have a slim chance of success on the north side, and yet we were determined to make a strong attempt. We had no idea what the lower 4,000 feet of our route would be like, not having photographs of this section. The pictures we did have showed the obviously difficult route we had chosen for the upper 8,000 feet. Now my view showed the true nature of the difficulties that awaited us. We finally knew what we were facing and I felt more sure of success than ever.

Jim appeared alongside me, then Lou, awestruck.

Jim was the first to break the silence. "God, that's impressive! That's our route right there!"

"We've got to send back for the fixed line we left in New Delhi," Lou said, eyeing us both.

"Well, if we hadn't given in to the others' arguments so easily, the rope would be here," I reminded him. "We're just damn lucky the rope's in New Delhi or you could kiss that route good-bye."

"How are we going to talk Willi into this one?" asked Jim. He was still thinking of Willi's ample powers of persuasion.

"The best way would be to let those who opposed fixed line convince him," Lou recommended.

Peter, the strongest opponent to fixed line, surmounted the ridge and joined us.

"Peter," I approached him, "the three of us think we're going to need the rest of the fixed line from New Delhi. Maybe John Evans could bring it in if we get a message out with Marty and the chopper. What do you think?"

Peter was obviously shocked at the mountain's sheerness.

"I hate to say it, gang, but I was wrong," Peter apologized. "We're going to need all the fixed line we have."

"Look," I began, "Jim and I have no credibility with the team right now. It's up to you to convince the others that we need to get the rest of the fixed line. We don't want to come off like 'We told you so.' If you can see the need, then there's no question we need the extra rope."

"O.K. I'll talk to Devi and Andy. Lou can help me out with a plan."

The issue was settled there. We would send back to New Delhi for the four thousand feet of rope we had left there.

Jim and I paced ourselves into the gorge to fix line for the porters while Lou and Pete stayed to convince the others of the necessity for additional rope. Peter's agreement was significant because he was a conversion. Elliot, Andy, then Devi came up and they also agreed the line was necessary. Willi was still down paying off the goat herders, so Devi volunteered to run down (two thousand feet) to Romani to tell him a message should be sent out with Ad and Marty. She felt she was the only one who could persuade Willi.

Devi was right. She had Willi's ear and, more important, respect. She could convince him where he might reject our arguments. According to her later, he didn't argue, just listened, considered some options with her, then sent a note out with the *bhakrawallas* for John Evans to bring the rope in. The team continued into the gorge with a little more peace of mind.

On July 21 the gorge seemed particularly beautiful. High clouds were slipping into the Sanctuary, hiding Nanda Devi's sharp summit, but the sun shone warm and comforting into the gorge. We passed rock slides of lichen-covered pink quartzite and knee-high juniper as we walked. Red and green rhubarb grew under overhanging cliffs and around the many small springs. Clumps of poplar clung precariously to the lower slopes in the gorge. Thick grass covered even the steepest areas, offering superb steps and handholds just in time for particularly bad sections of the trail. Jim and I stayed just ahead of the porters to Bujgara, the midway point through the gorge, and stopped for lunch.

The sweaty porters, who always dressed in the same layers of clothing whether the temperature was thirty or ninety degrees, quickly deposited their sixty-pound loads on the nearest relic campsite. Without stopping to rest, several of them turned downhill into a forested area to collect wood for their lunch fire. The rest of the Garhwalis mixed *atta* and water for *chapatis*. Lunch stops were usually an hour or two, involving lengthy cooking and a nap during the midday heat. But not today.

"Jim, we better get started," I said, suddenly realizing the porters were shouldering their loads.

"They're worried about the gorge today," Jim remarked as we quickly finished eating. "They must know something we don't."

They passed us as we packed, crossed the stream, and bunched up against a ten-foot wall on which hung a fluorescent red rope left by the recent Japanese expedition. Pushed from below, each porter took his turn surmounting the obstacle with plenty of help from his friends and the rope.

We helped the remaining porters, then struggled up ourselves. They stopped to rest and this gave Jim and me the opportunity to shoot out in front and continue fixing lines for them. The Japanese had fixed many of the dangerous sections and those that were marginally dangerous still had old propylene or manila rope from other parties.

Several areas were dangerous and difficult for the porters carrying the long, awkward boxes. At times a slip would have resulted either in a disastrous two-thousand-foot tumble to the Rishi or several broken bones in a minor fall.

The trail became less distinct and began to climb several vertical buttresses. Narrow cat tracks split the immense walls until we entered a gully after a short hand-and-toe traverse fixed with old manila rope. We waited as a few porters led the obscure trail, which climbed fifteen-foot vertical sections, at times on grass hummocks.

The fifteen-hundred-foot climb ended abruptly on a sloping plateau marked with two large cairns two hundred yards from our next camp, Pathal Khan. Suddenly we found ourselves free of the difficulties and dangers of the Rishi Gorge. Before us were the gradual slopes and easy paths of the inner Sanctuary. The months of anxiety I had felt over this day seemed far away. I could not concentrate on the climb itself.

The early afternoon heat was intense and we had passed little water to drink. A hazy cloud layer shielded little of the sun's ultraviolet rays as Jim and I sought some form of shelter and rest. Within a half hour, porters dropped into camp, left their loads, and sought shelter from the sun in cliffside caves above the campsite. The other sahibs filtered in slowly, exhausted and thirsty from the two-stage climb.

"I'm dying to go dunk my head in that stream," I thought aloud. "Care to go, Jim?"

"I'm right behind you!" he yelled, grabbing his towel and shampoo.

By the time Jim and I reached the stream a half mile from camp, Lou and Andy had already found a deep pool in which to soak their feet and wash.

"I think I frostbit my brain," Jim stuttered after pulling his head from the water, which two minutes before had been part of a glacier.

"How can that be?" I said. "Mountain climbers don't have brains."

"That's why we're here!" shouted Lou.

Like characters in the silent movies, we moved in jerks and spasms to avoid the dull ache of the icy water. Shadows stretched the length of the stream, pushing us into the scattered sunlight to stay warm. We soon had to dress and return to camp.

For most of the sahibs, camp meant meals, conversation, and rest. For Jim, it meant medical clinics for the porters. They had every conceivable medical problem, from amoebic livers to abscessed teeth. Jim would examine each man patiently, listening to the complaints through Kiran, the only interpreter.

The most common complaints were skin ailments, which were cured with soap, and eye infections, which the majority of Garhwalis had from living in smoky rooms. Their homes never had chimneys for the cook fires.

Jim often was discouraged. "They need more than I or any other physician can give them here. They need surgeons, hospitals, and permanent medical attention for some of these problems."

If one porter received a pink-and-green pill, there would be an influx of the medical problem that required that pill for several days. The more pills, and the more colorful the pills, the more the porters wanted them. Salt tablets were the standard medical cure-all for those porters with no ailment but who wanted a pill.

Five o'clock came early. *Chapatis* and oatmeal appeared through the door. Hot chocolate was served at the cook tent. The porters wanted an early start, although it was a short day to Sarson Patal, our intended Base Camp.

I started out of camp feeling great. But fifty yards onto the trail I slipped on a wet slab, sliding to a small ledge twenty feet below.

"Are you all right?" Jim asked.

"Damn! I hit my ankle and elbow. They're pretty banged up. I don't think anything's broken."

"Do you want me to check them out?"

"No, let's keep moving so the ankle stays loose, and I'll soak it at camp," I said.

The swollen ankle and bruised elbow were not the only casualties. My ego took a beating from the laughter of the twenty porters behind me. I could distinctly hear several say in broken English, "Very good, Sahib, very good."

The weather was still perfect. Jim and I followed the porters to the stream where the trail side-hilled back the same direction we had just come, but on the opposite side of the creek. We climbed steeply to a crest, then traversed along boulder fields of gray and pink quartzite. A large cairn marked a fork in the trail: one fork followed the north side of Nanda Devi, which we were to take; the other descended to the Rishi a thousand feet below, crossed on a makeshift rope bridge, and continued to the east toward the towering peaks of Kalenka and Changabang. We decided to eat and wait for the others.

All the sahibs sauntered in, stretched out in the warm sunshine, and added some form of food to the early lunch. Devi, Elliot, and Andy moved slowly, followed by Kiran and Nirmal. It had been days since we had all been together like this, able to enjoy one another's company. The mountain Nanda Devi stimulated a short discussion on our intended route but the beauty of the Sanctuary occupied everyone's mind.

"Jim, why don't you go on ahead? I'm going to take it slow for the afternoon." An overwhelming sense of lethargy blanketed me in the heat and moving ahead seemed futile.

"That sounds like my kind of trek, John. I want to enjoy this last bit."

Several large boulder fields led to the inner Sanctuary and a rainbow-colored meadow fed by a spring. Devi and Andy were relaxing alongside the stream in the deep grass when Jim, Lou, and I arrived. The stark contrast between the lifeless and hostile world of the mountain above and the warm, flowered meadow buzzing with insects where we sat left us quiet. Only the clicking of Jim's shutter broke the silence.

"I've never imagined her this beautiful." Devi gazed toward the mountain's summit slopes. "To think, tomorrow we will be climbing."

"Only if we can get all the gear sorted and repacked this afternoon," Andy commented. "We're still hoping the porters will carry at least to Advanced Base Camp and that's going to take some exploration of the route first."

Devi packed up and disappeared toward Base, alone, her white pajama bottoms waving in the stiff breeze. One could only guess what was in her thoughts. She had much more in her heart for Nanda Devi than did we.

The lower four thousand feet of Nanda Devi, a dark, shattered vertical wall of schists, slates, and dolomites, was soon fully visible. Nowhere along its entire length did it seem to offer the breach we so desperately needed to reach the upper face. Base Camp at 13,500 feet would be too low. We needed some moderate sections higher on the mountain to move the ton and a half of gear to within reasonable distance of the summit.

Base Camp was a mosaic pattern of four-foot-by-seven-foot excavated tent platforms torn from the lush green carpet of alpine grass and flowers. The encircled one large natural flat area that still retained portions of a rock shelter, perhaps used as a kitchen for other expeditions. A spring meandered through camp. Thick foliage along its banks ran in a crooked green strip along the barren soil. A rock monument, built by the Devistan Expedition, overlooked camp and the trail that continued around to the south side of Nanda Devi. Garbage littered a hundred square yards around camp. Old wick lanterns, blue propane Bleuet tanks, rusty cans, plastics, and old tennis shoes showed the lack of concern taken by previous expeditions for the remote environment of Nanda Devi.

A half mile below camp the newly born Rishi Ganga tore at the northwest flanks of Nanda Devi, which rose abruptly over twelve thousand feet to its top. Waterfalls cut the immense lower wall, slowly etching their paths through time, and helped by the constant rockfall we could hear from camp.

The wind tore at us in gusts as we descended into camp. Already the porters had gathered wood from the scrub brush of the stream gully and were cooking.

I was tired, my ankle and elbow throbbed, and my mood reflected the circumstances. The hike to base and the altitude had taken any remaining motivation from me. Jim, on the other hand, was obsessed with pitching the tents immediately. What was pushing Jim was not working on me or the others. Only guilt got us up and helping. The tents were finally found among the battered boxes, platforms releveled and cleaned, and our homes for the next few months pitched.

Jim's nervousness was apparent. He needed assurance that the route he had come so far to climb was worthwhile. He wasn't sure if Nanda Devi was worth leaving his practice and friends for, or if the mountain could fulfill his needs. The answer was a short walk up the hill and he didn't want to wait any longer to find it.

"Lou and I are going uphill to search out the route," Jim mentioned. "Do you want to go?"

"Why don't you relax?" I couldn't share their anxiety to search for a route through the lower maze. "Go ahead, I'll catch up."

When I finally caught them a half mile up the hill, they were scanning the lower slopes with binoculars.

"How does it look?" I asked. "Find any walk-ups?"

Neither of them answered.

Clouds had hidden the upper slopes, which made connecting the lower gullies to a feasible route above difficult.

"There's two possibilities John," Lou finally mumbled, keeping the binoculars to his eyes. "One is a gully a mile upstream. It looks like it could go through the wall, but I can't see it all the way. The other possibility is to climb the south side ridge and traverse all the way back along that upper ramp system four thousand feet up."

He handed me the glasses.

"I can see your gully, but only the first thousand feet. We need to get higher and farther over to see better."

"We can give it a try," Jim said, "but the creek is at high water."

The three of us tried to find a crossing point over a swollen, muddy brook from the Devistan Glacier far above, but it had grown impassable from the melting of miles of ice in the heat of the day. Discouraged with our lack of success, we retreated humbly to Base Camp.

"Hey, John!" It was Elliot. "Peter traversed into the Sanctuary real high and said the route looks bad."

"Really?" I made a beeline for Peter's tent.

Peter was one of America's most experienced altitude climbers. There weren't many in 1976. He had distinguished himself in Alaska on several major expeditions in the 1960s. He had also been with me on Dhaulagiri in 1973 and in the Russian Pamirs in 1974. Considered one of the top avalanche rangers and experts in the United States, he worked in avalanche control at Alta, Utah. His opinion was valuable.

Lou and Jim followed me into Peter's tent. Devi and Andy were already there.

"What did you see, Peter?" I asked.

"I don't want to say anything more." Discouragement lay heavy in his voice. The word had already spread that Peter didn't like the route above.

"I think it would be best for you to form your own opinion in the morning."

"You can't just leave us in suspense, Peter," Lou argued. "At least give us some indication of why you're so discouraged."

"We're experienced enough to judge for ourselves, Peter," I added. "Maybe you didn't see all the possibilities from where you viewed the face."

We finally got him to talk.

"I traversed into the Sanctuary at 15,000 feet and got a good view of the face," Peter began. He spoke slowly, studying what he said. "There is no way up the cliffs. Even if we could get up, we can't traverse above them. There is no plateau. The angle remains steep all the way up the face and the canyons cutting through the cliffs are impassable. The ice wall is really vertical."

Everyone had now heard the glum report. Our morale hung precariously.

"Walls always look vertical from head-on," I reminded him.

Lou continued. "Besides, Peter, from the distance you saw the face, there's no way you could see the minor features like ledges and good holds."

Devi attempted a positive note. "We didn't go around saying that we were coming over to do a particular route."

"We can be flexible," Elliot said.

"Bullshit!" I flared. "We came over here to do a new route and until we've exhausted every possibility, that's where we'll put our efforts."

Elliot was ready to walk out. Andy was undecided. Peter was very glum. Devi tried to cheer everyone up by saying we couldn't tell by first views, especially at this distance.

Willi later decided to send me and Lou, reputedly a level head, up the valley the next morning to reconnoiter a route to the upper slopes. The rest of the team would search for a better base camp closer to the mountain and climb high on the opposite slopes to get a better view of our intended route.

Seventeen days after arriving in New Delhi we were to be climbing. Lou and I rounded up a rope, some hardware, and our climbing equipment from the porter loads, ate an early dinner, and bedded down. I was too excited to sleep. What we had come so far to do was finally beginning.

FIVE

Lou and I took to the trail at 6:30 A.M., wondering why we had bothered to wait for our breakfast of oatmeal and *chapatis* that, as usual, sat like lead in our stomachs and had us searching for toilet tissue a half an hour down the trail.

The swollen torrent of yesterday gave us little trouble in the morning as we hopped several large boulders and scrambled up morainal debris on the other side to continue. A short hour's trek across the bouldered sidehills ended abruptly at the Rishi Ganga a mile downstream from its source, Nanda Devi's Southwest Glacier.

During the night the sky had become overcast and the thick clouds hung at barely two hundred feet. Our search for a route to the upper face would have to be hit or miss. We would have to follow each gully.

Although the day began badly with such a late start, our first good break occurred at the Rishi. Since the expedition began we had been concerned about crossing the Rishi without having to go clear to the south side of Nanda Devi, then crossing on the glacier and returning along the northwest bank. But the mountain itself provided the answer to this significant approach problem.

Small avalanches, formed in the powder snows ten thousand to twelve thousand feet above on Nanda Devi's Northwest Face, had gathered momentum on their descent and grown into monsters. The avalanches thundered the length of the face through large gullies to finally blast out onto the lower scree slopes and bridge the Rishi Ganga.

Blocked by tons of snow, the river had eaten its way through, forming a tunnel on its long journey to the sea. By this natural bridge of ice we crossed the river and knew by the avalanche debris which gully not to follow up the mountain.

We had one choice left. A single, deep, forty-foot-wide gully shot steeply upward and disappeared into the clouds. Neither Lou nor I expected this to be feasible for porters carrying loads, but there was nowhere else to go.

Climbing the gully was simple at first. Easy third-class scrambling from solid rock to loose, shingly scree tested our balance and prepared us for harder climbing above. We hugged the gigantic wall that disappeared above us until it was obvious the gully was a dead end. A traverse opened across dangerously loose rock to a narrow steep spine forming the backbone between two gullies. The one gully we had already ascended; the other was a dead end.

"This is going to be damn hard for porters, Lou."

"They can make it this far," he answered. "We may not get much farther beyond the top of this spine anyway. It looks like it peters out into that cliff a little higher up."

I scrambled up the sixty-degree ridge using the ample blocky holds. It was like crawling up a steep two-by-six plank atop a thirty-story building. A fixed line would definitely be needed for the porters. I reached the crest where the rib butted into a large wall.

"Lou!" I yelled. "I think we found the answer! There seems to be a narrow catwalk that will get us back into the gully and easier climbing."

He joined me at the top of the spine.

"This is the key alright," he said, breathing hard from the climb. "If the porters will come this far, we might get them to go all the way to the next camp."

A thirty-foot rock pitch, which would require another fixed line for the porters, and several hundred yards of easy traversing brought us to the center of a gully and a glacial run-off stream draining the Northwest Face. Above, it looked like safe, easy third-class scrambling. The approach to the upper face was solved.

"Everything seems to be falling into place," Lou remarked with surprise. "Now, if only we can find a suitable campsite for Advanced Base we'll be on our way."

"We're going to pick up everyone's enthusiasm with this news," I added. "When's radio call?"

"Another half hour yet. Let's go as far as we can up the gully before contact with the group to give them the most complete report on the route."

After a snack of *chapatis*, peanut butter, and jam, we scrambled up the right-hand slope of the stream. The altitude weighed heavy on us both, and we moved slowly in the thinner air. To find our way down and back up, we built large cairns—piles of stones—to designate important changes in our path. The route was too easy to believe.

At 10:00 A.M. Lou switched on the radio to make contact with Willi. He and the others were to search for a better base camp closer to our intended route while climbing higher opposite the Northwest Face in order to visually reconnoiter the upper slopes.

The morale of the climbers below had eroded even further. Jim, Willi, Andy, Devi, and Elliot had walked up and around the west buttress of the mountain, but couldn't see any possible break in Nanda Devi's defense. The poor visibility hadn't helped. Willi briefly described what he considered would be the route up higher on the mountain, but this required climbing under several icefalls high up. According to Jim, this depressed several climbers even more. Willi came across to them as justifying high risks in the Himalayas, and no one wanted to hear that. Jim recalled Elliot being concerned; Andy hesitantly supported Willi's ideas, and Devi preferred to watch and listen.

"Willi, this is Lou. Come in," Lou announced.

"We read you, Lou," Willi responded. "We've been waiting for your call. Where are you?"

"We're around 15,700 feet, Willi," Lou answered. "We've found a good route to the upper slopes and it looks like some really good spots for a camp up higher."

"Great!" The relief in Willi's voice was palpable. We could hear the others voicing similar relief in the background. "We're just opposite the ice bridge that crosses the Rishi. Where did you go up?"

Lou described the route in detail because they were still below the clouds and couldn't see where we had gone. Another radio call was scheduled in case we weren't down by 4:00 P.M., and Lou signed off.

Minutes later Lou and I were climbing steadily to our next goal, a broad ridge crest two thousand feet higher and toward an area of the face that looked feasible. For a thousand feet we meandered through short cliffs, scree, and boulders to the foot of a large snowfield, a relic of huge past avalanches. Even then small slides were coming down continuously, but they stopped far short of our position. The grating of sliding snow sounded so close in the fog that we panicked, scrambling off to the sides of the gully. No avalanche ever came close but our fear was compounded by our inability to see through the dense fog.

We climbed the rock alongside the avalanche debris for four hundred feet before crossing to the other side. From there we found an easy ascent to the ridge crest. The crest's broad spine formed a thousand feet above us and ended in a blank wall at the Rishi, thirty-five-hundred feet below. Our campsite, later known as "Ridge Camp," seemed well protected from avalanche and rockfall. Snow and debris would most likely go into gigantic gullies on either side. It was an excellent spot for an intermediate camp before we would need a camp closer to our intended route.

At this altitude the mountain's bands of loose mica schist and brown flagstone provided flat and easily excavated campsites all along the Northwest Face. Although treacherously rotten and platey, these bands made it much easier to traverse to our intended advanced base a half mile away to the east, but only a few hundred feet higher.

Below us, the ridge narrowed into a blade knifing the sky, stabbing at Mt. Devistan on the outer rim of the Sanctuary. From the point of the blade, it plummeted in hundred-foot tiers to the Rishi far below.

"This will be an excellent dropping place for the loads," Lou decided. "From here we can have carries to that ridge over there." He pointed to another broad rib across the Northwest Glacier. "That will probably be a perfect spot for Advanced Base."

"I don't like traversing under that big glacier," I added, "but I guess there's not too much debris underneath . . ."

"Yeah, but something had to create those snow bridges over the Rishi below," Lou added.

I started building a large cairn while Lou found a decent privy. We relaxed for several hours to acclimatize to the new altitude before descending the gully. The route seemed even easier going down than it had on the ascent. I was sure the porters could do it. Our only problems now would be the weather and the porters' willingness to carry. The first was up to God, the second to Kiran. Each, I believed, was qualified to handle his end.

Lou and I returned early and discussed with the group why Peter had felt that the route would not go. He just hadn't gained enough altitude the day before to view the upper slopes without distortion.

"Jim, I tell you, the campsites are as big as football fields." I exaggerated for effect. "You can play frisbee up there!"

Lou continued to answer Willi's questions until everything was clear. "Not only did we find suitable campsites, but we got a good view of the upper face and it's only forty to forty-five degrees at the most!"

"You guys did a great job," Willi said. "This is going to put us ahead by at least a week."

Not everyone was convinced. "I would like to go up tomorrow and see for myself," Peter demanded. "I'd feel more confident."

Peter, one of the most experienced climbers on the team, had to see the route for himself. As an avalanche ranger, he needed his own assurance that the route was clear of the avalanches that would consume the mountain in the coming monsoon. I had a lot of respect for his opinion. But after the incident at Dibrugheta, I was not about to tolerate any resistance to this route.

"O.K.," Willi agreed. "Why don't you and Lou fix

lines in the worst area for the porters and the rest of us will guide them to the ridge?''

''We've got to organize the food tonight then,'' Elliot pointed out. ''Everybody will have to help so the porters can carry tomorrow.''

Although young and inexperienced, Elliot knew that the porters had to be satisfied with the weight of the loads if we expected them to carry over difficult terrain. Up to this point he had said little, but I suspected he would follow Willi's lead in any discussion. Now he was anxious to get on with the climb as if all the indecision made him nervous. I still didn't know how to take Elliot. He still looked sixteen. I was curious about his history with Ad that qualified him to be invited on such a prestigious expedition. After all, Ad had access to a lot of good climbers in the U.S., yet here was Elliot.

While Lou and I were on the mountain, the others had also been busy. They had walked the several miles to the Japanese base camp site and found porter food left by the Japanese—enough for us to keep our porters several more days. In that time they could help us establish a solid camp high on the mountain. Base Camp soon became a warehouse of open boxes and flapping plastic bags as the food list was read off and each item was found, measured, and tossed into eight-man-day unit piles.

''Devi, you and I can separate the powdered milk, freeze-dried potatoes, and salt,'' Elliot said, ''while Lou and Andy put the candy and cookies into piles. Peter, you can help with the potatoes and noodles.''

Willi, Jim, and I tried hiding in our tents to write a last letter before going up the mountain, but Devi quickly shamed us into helping.

''John, how would you like to rebag the tea?'' Devi asked. ''Here, I've got the tea and bags right here with me.''

''How much do I put in each . . . ?'' It was no use. She was gone, leaving me to do my share.

Jim was annoyed because he had to sort Gumperts drink mix, so I went back to my tent for peace and quiet. No sooner would I finish one food than Devi would hand me another to rebag.

Willi was tossing crackers into piles as I finished my short job. "John, there's still candy to repack. Want to do it?" he asked. "Andy is doing some sorting in the tent, but there are more boxes of hard candy and chocolate over there."

Devi found Jim writing in his tent and gave him the job of packaging cornuts. Kiran and Nirmal worked on stick jerky, a food they, as Hindus, couldn't even eat.

By the time the eight-man-day units were finished, each bag weighed thirty-three pounds. Willi fished through each sack and removed various amounts of candy, crackers, jello, and noodles to limit the weight of each unit to approximately thirty pounds. We still weren't through.

Porter loads had to be made up, each one limited to forty-five pounds because of the difficulty and altitude of the carry to Ridge Camp. Nirmal weighed each package under the close scrutiny of Jagatsingh. All seemed acceptable.

That evening we heard news from the outside world for the first time. The BBC drifted in and out over our cheap Indian radio, but we did learn the U.S. had captured the most medals in the summer Olympics at Montreal after three days of competition. After the news Nirmal usurped the radio and entertained us the rest of the evening with loud Indian music.

A beautiful dawn greeted us on July 24. Lou and Peter had disappeared into the early morning mist long before the rest of us left the security of our down bags.

"Surrendra!" I yelled, walking toward the kitchen. "Breakfast ready?"

"Yes, Sahib." Surrendra held out a plate of *parathas*, a *ghee*-fried *chapati*, and motioned for me to help myself to the mush still bubbling in the pot over the small fire.

"Hey Willi, what's going on?" I asked, noticing all the porters sitting on a sidehill above camp. Kiran was gesturing and arguing with Jagatsingh in front of them all, his Hindi rising in pitch as the discussion progressed.

"The porters want to be paid for their carries to here right now," he answered. "Kiran thinks if we pay them now they won't carry up the gully today. He's going to argue with them."

I ate breakfast slowly and then packed for the climb to Ridge Camp. The other sahibs gathered around their tents to listen and wait for the outcome. The heated voices of several porters said they weren't going anywhere. I leaned toward the porters' side of the issue, and so stayed out of the argument.

"Andy, notice those two young porters on the right side?" I asked. "They seem to be the troublemakers."

"I've been watching . . . Most of them don't seem worried about the whole thing," Andy observed. "They're just sitting back and letting a few of the hotheads fight it out."

I had just about given up going anywhere for the day when, simultaneously, every porter jumped to his feet, grabbed his load, and trotted down the trail. I had no time to lose.

There were no other sahibs ready to go, so I threw my pack on and went after the disappearing porters. I was the only one who knew where to take them.

"Who in the hell is leading these guys?" I thought to myself, trying to keep pace with the last of the porters. Traveling without their normal stops, we were soon three hundred feet above the avalanche bridge over the Rishi. I was nearly exhausted.

The porter who had led the dash to this point was stopped in front of me, dripping sweat, smiling from ear to ear. He was obviously sure that I would drop from exhaustion and only his elfish grin stopped me from doing so. Kesharsingh's took of supremacy was firmly placed in my mind. I couldn't stop now.

Gathering every ounce of energy I had left, I continued on without stopping, trying to appear concerned about the gully and not about collapsing where I stood.

"You're a very strong porter." I tried to say the sentence to the grinning Keshar without sounding breathless as I passed. I think he was impressed.

By now all the porters were watching. I needed to get out of their sight to stop, but the nearest hiding spot was four hundred vertical feet away. I kept going. Fifteen feet more, ten, five, and I was hidden!

Every muscle was throbbing, especially the one between my ears. I dropped to my knees, quivering. My lungs burned.

"That was dumb, real dumb," I mumbled to myself.

The porters, led by my tormentor, began climbing the gully in a close-knit group to avoid kicking rocks on one another. The climb to the upper five hundred feet of the gully to the cul-de-sac was difficult in the deep, loose scree. I crossed the gully at its head to a two-hundred-foot eighty-degree wall where Peter and Lou had strung the first fixed line. With delicate steps I climbed the wall, using the rope for protection and help.

"No! Up here!" I yelled. "Fixed line! See?" I held up the line for the porters to see.

It was no use. They crossed the gully low down where Lou and I had gone the day before. They would surely balk at having to climb fourth- and easy fifth-class rock with those awkward loads.

As soon as I topped out on the spine of the ridge, I dropped my load and descended the rib to the now-transfixed porters. They were definitely not pleased with the route before them.

"No, Sahib," one of the troublemakers said. "No good!" He motioned at his load and at the route, then shook his head in finality.

Others began discussing the situation in Garhwali. They were scared.

"O.K., listen. Only this part bad, but very short," I demonstrated with my hands. "Good holds, see?"

I wasn't convincing. All the porters were now on the rib's platform. While some voiced their disgust, others sat back to listen and wait. Seldom would one porter make a different decision when there was dissension among the group.

"All right, any porter who carries to Ridge Camp," I pointed in the general direction, "gets five more rupees." Five fingers and the word "rupees" got the point across.

There was a short discussion and several of the stronger

porters picked up their loads and began following me up the difficult rib.

These were superb mountaineers. Their balance and coordination were perfect despite the ungainly loads. I saw several more retreat to the gully and climb up the fixed line. Only a few left their loads and returned to camp.

We arrived at my pack within ten minutes. I couldn't believe that some of them had just come up unroped, heavily loaded, and with horrible footwear. I waited patiently for everyone to appear, then followed several of the sturdiest porters along the catwalk beneath the thousand-foot vertical wall. A fixed line hung from one more short vertical step, then we reached the stream crossing. The porters stopped for a break and again started worrying about the route.

"There is no more danger. Very easy from here," I explained through gestures, punctuating each sentence loudly with "five rupees."

A timely bit of rockfall into the streambed convinced them quickly to move ahead. Some power higher than I was surely helping out.

Each porter swung across a slab on another short fixed section and continued up a slope that may as well have been marbles.

"I don't believe this! You can't stop here!" I was starting to lose my patience. They only wanted to eat lunch. "*Chapatis*, Sahib?"

Jim emerged, approaching my group of stagnant porters from below. "How are things going, John?"

"The porters keep stopping and complaining," I said. "I don't know if they'll go all the way."

"Look, Surrendra and I will keep going," Jim offered, "and maybe that will shame them into following."

"O.K., I'll keep shoving them from behind."

After lunch the porters balked again. Several felt five rupees was not worth the danger. All went another hundred yards, dropped their loads, and quit. I couldn't blame them. Then they started asking for pills for headaches caused by the altitude.

"When you get to camp above, I will pass out headache pills," Jim promised.

I sat back and watched, beaten and argued out. I was emotionally drained and had nothing else to say. The strong porter named Keshar said something to the remaining porters who hadn't as yet headed down. He must have said he was going up, because he shouldered his load and began the climb to Ridge Camp. The remaining porters followed.

They were determined now to make the ridge. They were going all the way. I pushed myself hard to catch Kesharsingh. He was a tiger. We raced past Jim and Surrendra, crossed the avalanche, and drove hard for camp.

Throughout all my travels, never had I come across one who had shown a desire to compete for competition's sake like Keshar. He didn't want me to pass him and tried to stay ahead of me, driving us both to collapse. Neither of us would give in.

My temples throbbed, sweat dripped into my eyes, along my ears, down my neck, into my mouth. My calves burned from pushing to stay with this steam engine of a man in front. I thought my ribs would crack.

Thank God he's slowing, I thought, as, from the corner of my eye, I saw Keshar relax slightly. This gave me the chance to push straight up and into the lead. I never gave it up.

I stumbled into Ridge Camp at 17,000 feet, all but passed out from exertion. Keshar was on my heels. He was still grinning, but visibly done in. We both put down our loads and laughed, slapping each other on the shoulders.

"Nome?" I asked in Hindi.

"Ah, Kesharsingh," he replied. *"Nome?"* He pointed at me.

"John," I answered.

"John Sahib?"

"No, Keshar. John."

He smiled happily, "Yes, John."

We were friends.

Keshar hefted his load, then mine. A smile as broad as

a river crossed his lips. My load was five pounds lighter than his. He jokingly disapproved.

"I want you to stay with the expedition, Keshar," I said, "as a high-altitude porter. Understand?"

He wasn't sure if he wanted to be away from his farm that long but he didn't say no. Several minutes later Jim arrived hungry but elated.

"Wow, what a place!"

"Lou and Peter are crossing the gully under the Northwest Face," I pointed out. "Looks like they got to Advanced Base on that other ridge."

"The route above looks a lot safer than I expected. Hardly suicidal," Jim added.

Of the fifty porters who had started from Base Camp, only twenty-three made it to Ridge Camp. Twenty-one had quit in the first gully, six had abandoned their loads somewhere in between. I felt lucky we got as many up as we had.

Jim was surrounded immediately by porters demanding pills to relieve their headaches.

"As soon as you drop your load go down to camp," Jim requested. None of them moved. "They can't understand, John."

"I maybe help," said one porter. "I speak some English."

"Better than our Garhwali," I pointed out. "What's your name?"

"Balbirsingh, Sahib," he answered quietly.

Balbir was of Tibetan origin. He had midnight black hair and oriental eyes of the same color. At five-feet eight-inches, he was tall compared to the average Garhwali. His English was definitely a strong point in favor of keeping him for the rest of the trip.

"O.K., Balbir," Jim said, "tell them after they take one of these pills to go down quickly. O.K.?"

Balbir seemed to get the idea and translated Jim's request. Each porter took a long red pill and waited, not making a move to descend.

"O.K., you guys," I growled, "get moving!" I shoved a few of them down toward Base. They got the hint.

"Jim, that was a funny-looking pill for a headache," I remarked. "What was it really for?"

"Oh, I didn't have aspirin, so I gave them my vitamin pills." We both broke into laughter.

"How did it go?" I asked Lou as he climbed toward us.

"Good," he said, breathless. "The route to Advanced Base is easy. We found a campsite that is flat and right on the top of the ridge. We shouldn't have any trouble setting up tents and establishing a secure camp."

"Did you get a glimpse of the route above?" Jim asked.

"It looks pretty straightforward up the ridge to the next camp," Lou guessed. "After that we'll have to venture out onto the slopes and gullies of the North Face. Hopefully we'll be able to hide under cliffs and climb ribs to avoid the avalanches. At any rate, the technical difficulties are minor compared to that huge buttress underneath the summit area. That's going to be yours, Roskelley."

"We'll see when we get there," I replied.

"How do you feel about the route now, Peter?" Jim asked.

"It doesn't look too bad," he agreed. "We carried under the glacier. There's only about fifteen feet of ice to cross. The porters won't have any trouble at all."

The four of us sat and talked for a while longer.

"You know, Elliot told me this morning he wanted to go home," Jim said.

"Yeah," Peter added, "Elliot's been talking like that for several days now. He's said the same thing to me, too."

"What's his problem?" I asked.

"He just doesn't want to be here," Jim answered. "He feels it's too dangerous and he keeps joking halfheartedly about getting killed on the face."

"This type of thing could snowball," I added.

"I'll work on helping him out," Jim volunteered, "but everyone should be aware of the problem."

None of the other sahibs appeared, so the four of us trotted, jumped, and skidded down the thirty-five-hundred-foot gully. One hour and eighteen minutes later I walked into Base Camp a short distance ahead of the others. By now Ad had arrived at Base Camp after seeing Marty flown out.

"Ad! You made it!" I reached for his hand. "Where's Marty? Did she get out O.K.? How was she feeling?"

"It's good to be here," he replied. "Marty was helicoptered out two days ago, on the twenty-first. She was feeling better, but was really tired. She slept for twenty hours straight on the last day."

Jim, Peter, and Lou entered camp and greeted Ad with the same questions. Although cheered by Ad's arrival, we were all bitterly disappointed—still no mail and no word from John Evans. Both were becoming extremely crucial to our morale. After dinner Willi and Ad called a team meeting.

"You've all heard the good news of Marty's evacuation," Ad began. "I firmly believe it was the best decision, taking into account the symptoms she still had the last few days."

The group was silent as each person entertained his own thoughts of Dibrugheta.

"To this point we are financially better off than I thought we would be," Ad reported. "Of the seven thousand dollars cashed into rupees, we have spent only three thousand dollars, and all but a few major expenses have been taken care of."

Hoots and hollers filled the tent with this news.

Willi continued, "There's one important item I feel needs mention here. Ad has decided his usefulness to the expedition is over at this point and has decided to leave the Sanctuary in a week or two. I think we owe him a great deal of thanks for doing such a superb job."

"You can't leave, Ad!"

"There's plenty to keep you busy between here and the lower camps."

"Please stay, Ad."

No one wanted to see him leave. Elliot just stared at the floor. His desire to quit the mountain became greater with every development of this kind. The meeting adjourned in twilight.

Lou and I were to move up and occupy Ridge Camp the next morning and establish Advanced Base Camp with tents and food in the next few days. The others would make several more carries and occupy Ridge Camp two or three days later.

Peter was particularly sensitive about who moved up to Ridge Camp. He expressed his concern to Lou that both Lou and I, who were strong anyway, would get in front of the group and stay in front. Lou assured him that this was not to be the case.

The Peter we had known as helpful and conscientious on other trips had become another man. He had been depressed since Dibrugheta. He seemed to have deep-seated suspicions of Jim, Lou, and me, as if our motives in climbing Nanda Devi were different from his. I considered our move to Advanced Base a reward for our enthusiasm, but Peter took this as a sign of our strength—not only physically, but in the team's hierarchy as well. I knew that our move was only temporary because the others would soon move up to take our places. I personally looked forward to the change of route leaders so I could climb again with Jim higher up. Peter had expressed a desire to be his own boss on this expedition. Only the expedition would suffer.

My pack the next morning was heavy—well over sixty pounds—for the carry to Ridge Camp. I wanted to be sure that if Keshar lifted it again he wouldn't laugh. Although desperately loaded, I was now familiar with the route and after three-and-a-half hours I arrived at Ridge Camp, minutes before a heavy rain began.

The porters, who at first refused to carry again, decided after talking to Keshar and Kiran that the trail was not so bad after all and all carried that day. Those who had dropped their loads down low the day before found them and carried them the rest of the way.

"Lou, we can't continue to Advanced Base today," I said as he arrived at the ridge. "We don't have the master list of the gear. How will we separate food and cooking equipment from the cache?"

"Andy's got the list. When he gets here, we'll find

what we need, but we should stay here at Ridge." The steady downpour had convinced him.

Andy and Devi entered camp dripping wet. Although uncomfortable, Devi couldn't get over just being there for the first time. The four of us erected a four-man tent and scurried inside to wait out the storm.

"Do you have the list of what's in the boxes Andy?" Lou asked.

"What list was that?" Andy asked, puzzled. "I don't have any list."

"Damn, another foul up," I said. "Maybe we can have Elliot read it to us over the radio at six o'clock. Meanwhile, we can dig around in the boxes for something to eat and cook with."

Willi, Kiran, Surrendra, and Jatendra appeared out of the dense mist below.

"Beautiful day John. Great carry!" Nothing could destroy Willi's youthful enthusiasm. I liked Willi. I saw his drive and success as similar to my own—he was a part of me in a white beard and laughing eyes. We would have made an invincible partnership had we been of the same generation.

However, Surrendra and Jatendra, the two IMF trainees, were a great disappointment to me. Neither seemed willing to work hard; Jatendra had not carried for several days because of a sore throat. During a team meeting the previous night, I had argued to send them out and keep Kesharsingh and Balbirsingh, who were much stronger and more willing to work. I also liked them much better as companions.

The other climbers opposed me. Willi and Ad argued that we hadn't paid insurance for Keshar and Balbir and it was not known whether we could at this late date. Besides, Surrendra and Jatendra had been supposedly doing their jobs.

"Not as far as I'm concerned," I argued. "I've been with them when they've carried and they weren't trying hard. We've given them all new equipment and now that they've got it, they've eased up. They're certainly not as tough as Keshar and Balbir."

Kiran and Nirmal, slightly embarrassed, came to their

protegés' defense. "They are good chaps," insisted Kiran in his strong, accented English. "You'll see. I will make them work bloody hard!"

Kiran's word was enough for me. The issue was settled by keeping all four of them, plus another strong porter from Lata. I was satisfied.

Willi, Kiran, and the two high-altitude porters joined us in the tent to escape the rain. Nirmal and most of the porters had already started down and I could see Jim and Elliot far below still climbing in the mist.

The tent had become a muddy mess when I finally reentered. Andy and Devi wanted to stay overnight because of the rain, but with the arrival of Willi and Kiran, Andy's argument to stay fell on deaf ears. Willi told them all to return to Base Camp. Lou and I had been looking forward to breaking off from the main group for a few days, so we were relieved.

With Willi's persuasion and a slowing of the rain, Andy and Devi reluctantly got ready to leave. Low on the horizon, the sun shone through the heavy clouds and sparkled off the wet slate like diamonds.

I was bending over tying my shoelace when I heard a vaguely familiar ape-like grunt from behind me.

I turned around. "What the hell are you doing, Devi?"

Like a monkey with bowlegs and drooped arms, Devi was uttering *"Ooh, Ooh, Ooh,"* as she did in wrestling matches with her brothers. Willi, Lou, and Andy started watching. Grinning devilishly, she began to approach me.

"Quit playing around, Devi," I ordered, feeling a little annoyed at this game and slightly uneasy at the thought she might not be kidding.

"SCREECH!"

She leapt upon me, bowling me over into the mud and rock. I couldn't believe what she had just done and sat there for several seconds while she mauled me. Instinct had me on my hands and knees with Devi still on top of me. With a twist, I pinned her by the shoulders to the ground.

"What's come over you?" I asked, breathless.

Smiling but breathing hard she replied, "Just having fun."

Willi and Andy laughed heartily. They congratulated Devi for taking me down a notch from the pedestal they felt I had put myself on throughout the trip. Only then did I realize that Devi had just demonstrated her displeasure at my insistence that she and Andy return to Base Camp. My butt hurt from the first grounding and my ego was a bit deflated.

"Hey, I'm sorry I got mad Devi," I apologized sheepishly.

"Next time I'll beat ya!" she said, laughing. Waving good-bye, she and the other four descended for Base.

Jim and Elliot arrived minutes later, soaked to the skin, but still enthusiastic. Jim put a little more joy into his voice for Elliot's sake.

"What did I tell you, Elliot," Jim exclaimed. "Isn't it fantastic, really something?"

Elliot wasn't impressed. "It looks dangerous to me, but maybe I'll get into it soon."

His mood was depressing. The three of us glanced at one another while Elliot looked around. Jim must have read my thoughts.

"Be careful what you say to him John," Jim warned. "He's talked about nothing but going home the entire day . . . but maybe getting here will help him change his mind."

"Maybe it would be best for us and him if he did leave," I suggested. "He's lowering everyone's morale with his indecision."

Jim was aware of the problem. "Let's get everybody as high on the mountain as we can, as soon as possible, before they change their minds. Peter's morale is hurting too."

Elliot and Jim descended, leaving Lou and me to spend the night at Ridge Camp. Hunger drove us into every box looking for food, pots, and a stove. We found shrimp, jerky, crackers, and Tang, the perfect antidote for Lou's constant diarrhea.

During the 7:00 P.M. radio call that night the decision to keep the five high-altitude porters was made. It had become a nasty issue. Nirmal had brought Jatendra and Surrendra from the IMF school where he was an instructor. He would lose face if they didn't stay. On the other hand, I wanted the best men available and made my choice based on their performance. Lou and Jim agreed with me. The sahibs' poor record of carrying up to this point dictated we keep the five men.

The next morning the weather was worse, alternating rain and snow. At 7:00 A.M. Willi made radio contact and informed us no one would be coming to Ridge Camp because of the hammering rain.

"That's fine," Lou acknowledged, "anything else?"

"Yeah, Lou . . ." Willi's voice crackled over the radio, "the team voted you as climbing leader instead of John Evans. Congratulations from all of us."

"Me?!" Lou stammered. "O.K., but only until Evans arrives."

"O.K.," Willi agreed. "We're going to sign postcards for our contributors today. Wish you were here."

"Forge our names, will you?" Lou kidded.

We dressed and packed loads for a carry to the Advanced Base site. I put on my fourteen-pound, size 12½-double boots for the first time and had the feeling I was chained to one spot. A scree slope led down a short gully where we traversed two hundred yards to the beginning of the quarter-mile crossing underneath the Northwest Glacier.

"This place gives me the creeps," I muttered, glancing up. The snout of the glacier was notched in the center from the scouring of small avalanches.

Hurriedly we crossed, then climbed to a large level spot on a ridge crest, slightly higher than Ridge Camp a half mile across from us. Leveling a tent platform proved easy and soon we were out of the rain and eating our lunches.

"We better get back across," Lou said. "The temperature's risen and this could bring down some of the snow that's been falling up high."

We realized we hadn't fully acclimatized yet as we struggled back up to Ridge Camp an hour later. No avalanches came during our crossing. A good sign for the future, we thought. Lou succumbed to another attack of diarrhea while I sacked out for a long nap.

The weather deteriorated that afternoon. Slushy snow

and rain pounded the mountain, creating a quagmire around the tent. Small avalanches scraped along in both gullies on either side of us. We could only hear them through the thick clouds enveloping our camp. Rockfall from directly above came too close for us to relax.

"Hear that?" I whispered.

"Yeah," Lou said, eyeing me in fear. "I think it's coming this way!"

I leapt for the tent door and stared up hopelessly into the mist. "It's going to miss us. They just sound like they're coming through the tent. I don't believe rocks can hit us here."

The afternoon passed slowly. Lou cooked Japanese noodles and raspberry custard for dinner, but neither of us could unwind.

Down at Base Camp, Willi, Ad, and Kiran paid off the porters, who were glad to be going home. Some were told to return for us when we needed them. They had performed well on incredibly difficult terrain while under very awkward loads—a tribute to their toughness and loyalty.

"Come in, Base," Lou called over the radio.

Willi responded, but before Lou could answer, an enormous avalanche broke free of the Northwest Face and swept the quarter-mile gully that we had crossed that morning. The onslaught lasted fifteen minutes.

"Did you hear that, Willi?" Lou cried. "That avalanche had to go clear to the Rishi!"

"We heard it alright. Everything O.K. up there?"

Although scared, we weren't in danger of being swept away. An hour later another one of similar size slid through the gully. The warm air and heavy snows high up had created the perfect conditions for the monster avalanches. All night smaller avalanches cascaded down the once-peaceful gully and swept our crossing point. Never again during the next six weeks did we feel safe carrying to Advanced Base.

The mountain continued to convulse violently while we waited out the weather at the lonely Ridge Camp. This was a wild and hostile place, yet serene; only nature's sounds interrupted the silence. But the mountain's beauty was clouded by fear—fear of dying, of hurting others, of the unknown.

The weather continued to defy us. The rain had changed to a misty drizzle; a slight wind had risen. Willi told us that Jim and Elliot would be coming up to stay and to occupy Advanced Base with us the next day.

Lou and I began ferrying loads at around 8:00 A.M. It didn't take us long to reach the debris of yesterday's avalanches.

"Those babies were bigger than I thought. This doesn't look like the same mountain!" I said.

The entire gully, over a quarter mile wide, was buried with deep piles and blocks of debris. What had been easy walking along tiers of rock the day before was now a frozen river of snow and ice.

"We can't get caught in the middle of the gully with something that big coming," warned Lou, shaking his head. "We're going to have to be more careful crossing this spot day after day."

Crossing now seemed suicidal because of the warm air and continuing rain, but it was still early in the morning. Everything higher might still be frozen.

"Let's give it a go, Lou."

We made a dash for the other side, but it still took us a full ten minutes, leaving us breathless and exhausted on the other side. Neither of us could concentrate on picking a good route for fear of seeing another avalanche come over the lip of the glacier.

"Here comes one," I yelled. "Run for it!"

We started to move quickly, then suddenly I realized the sound was coming from underneath. It was only the muffled roar of a stream under the avalanche debris.

We collapsed on the other side, dumped our loads, and dashed back. We carried to the edge of the glacier two more times that day, all the while feeling doom was impending, and left our loads at a cache site alongside the glacier instead of taking them across. It was a frightening spot. The monsoon was showing its teeth. The expedition would have to face the humid heat and heavy snows for the rest of the trip.

Elliot and Jim met us that afternoon with the eight remaining porters.

"Those avalanches last night crossed the Rishi and left thousands of tons of snow down there," Elliot said. "An avalanche that size could have wiped out a city!"

"Elliot," Lou said, "you and Jim can have the first leads to Camp I as soon as we get to Advanced Base. How does that sound?"

"If I get there, I'd like to," he agreed.

Elliot seemed a little more at ease and prepared a superb dinner of pork chops, noodles, and pudding. The weather looked better as we crawled into our sleeping bags. Only the avalanches disturbed our slumber, creating panic late into the night.

In the morning it was my turn to feel the paralysis of fear.

"I'm psyched out, guys," I confessed. "It's too warm . . . something's going to break loose today. It avalanched all night. I don't think I'm going to cross that glacier today."

Everyone felt the same tension.

After a brief radio call, during which Lou recommended no one carry from below, the four of us dressed, shouldered our gear, and descended to the gully.

"Who's going to cross?" Lou asked.

Jim, Elliot, and I, fearing the worst, decided not to go. Lou, determined to show Elliot there was nothing to fear, forged across.

Lou later wrote to his wife: "I made the crossing mostly to show Elliot it could be done. I felt pretty exposed doing it, though. Coming back was particularly difficult mentally."

Elliot wasn't impressed and withdrew within himself even further.

I carried down to the gully alone an hour later, ashamed of myself for not forging ahead that morning with Lou. I made the crossing and returned to camp with some dubious self-respect restored.

The four of us carried four more times to the edge of the gully that day. The more gear we could transfer, the less work there would be later for the others. To our surprise, Andy, Devi, Nirmal, Kiran, Peter, and Surrendra arrived at Ridge Camp late that afternoon.

While several of us built a platform for their four-man tent, the new arrivals relaxed after the long carry from Base. Devi was her usual energetic self, bustling about camp, rummaging through boxes for cooking equipment and coming up with different foods as well. Surrendra built an enclosure from the porter loads and spread a rain tarp over the stacked boxes for a kitchen and sleeping area. The porters had brought wood for cooking up to Ridge and Advanced Base camps.

This unexpected influx of people depressed me. The peace and quiet of the camp had disappeared. I found a beautiful spot on the tip of the ridge below camp and retreated for the afternoon.

Kiran disappeared into his tent, while Nirmal felt more comfortable with Surrendra under the kitchen tarp. When things had quieted down, I returned to camp for my camera and walked uphill. Peter joined me a short time later. Our conversation was alarming.

"I'm going to carry loads only when I want," he stated flatly. "I respect Lou's judgment, but I'm not taking orders from anybody about when or where I carry."

"Lou's the climbing leader, Peter," I argued, irritated with his attitude. "We all have to work as a unit, not separately. We'll never climb this peak if we all carry when we feel like it." I got up and returned to camp, annoyed.

Devi cooked a superb dinner. The nine sahibs sacked out in the two tents while Surrendra nestled under his cook tarp. Jim didn't like the separation of sahibs and porters.

"Hell, you discouraged him from sleeping in here," Jim said. "This is damned unfair of us."

"Jim, Surrendra has been sleeping with the other porters and is bound to have lice," I explained. "Sure it's unfair, but I don't want to host some parasite throughout the entire climb. We've got enough problems just with the route."

This satisfied him for the time being. Everyone fell

asleep to the patter of rain on the tent roof and the hourly rumble of avalanches.

"Ready to go across today, Elliot?" Lou asked the next morning. Wet snow was still falling, blanketing the camp.

"We'll see when I get down there," Elliot replied.

Suddenly Jim jumped on Elliot to wrestle playfully and release some tension. Lou and I moved out of the way as they rolled and grappled around the tent. But Elliot wrestled as if for his life. Jim had to fight hard to keep Elliot from pinning him. Jim finally overcame Elliot's effort.

Everyone in the tent could feel the angry charge in the air. Elliot seemed to fall into an even deeper emotional quandary than before. He dressed and disappeared out the tent door. After breakfast, those who wanted to carry across the glacier with Jim, Lou, Elliot, and me loaded their packs with food and climbing gear and descended with us to the gully's edge.

Our nerves were taut at having to cross. The chances of an avalanche were even greater with the warm weather and heavy snowfall of the past night.

Elliot sat down at the cache. He stared across the gully, then stood up again. The terrible indecision distorted his young face. He seemed to age years in moments. There was nothing we could say to help our friend make his decision.

Lou started across.

"I hope to see you on the other side, Elliot," I said as I picked up my pack and followed Lou into the drizzle and under the deadly Northwest Face. I was scared too.

Jim, Peter, and then Devi followed, leaving Elliot to struggle with himself alone. Once across, Jim did the unexpected.

"I dropped my load on the other side," Jim recalled, "and felt as though I should do the best I could for Elliot. So I crossed back over the glacier to talk to him. I moved fast because the sun was coming out and I felt that an avalanche would come, but none did.

"I sat down beside Elliot and he was crying, really torn. He wanted me to hold him for a while. I leaned over, put my arms around him, and told him I had crossed back over just to get him. He still wouldn't come. I pleaded with him, saying I really cared about him. Finally the air temperature was getting too warm and I had to cross. I finally told him to do what he thought best."

Peter and Devi reached Elliot as Jim began the long, lonely journey to where Lou and I waited on the other side.

"Couldn't talk him into coming?" I asked.

"No," Jim looked me in the eye, "and I don't think he will, either."

It was a sad picture. At the same time, I couldn't help feeling a little relief knowing I wouldn't have to hold my tongue anymore. We had all been tiptoeing around Elliot as if he would explode at the mention of danger.

Jim, Lou, and I climbed to the tent Lou and I had pitched several days before, unloaded our packs, and relaxed. Advanced Base was finally occupied.

At midday, Kiran, Nirmal, and Surrendra risked the avalanche danger and carried their loads to Advanced Base.

They acted uneasy at the campsite and seemed to search about for something. Kiran broke their awkward silence.

"Nirmal and I think this is a dangerous campsite," he said softly. "It would be safer from rockfall if it were several hundred yards lower down behind those short walls."

We looked around our flat, open campsite and realized the craters in the scree were from large boulders hitting the ridge from long distances and great height. Sheepishly, we agreed to move the camp.

With their help, Jim and I pitched two tents where they recommended, while Lou descended to pick up a load at the glacier's crossing point. Our Indian teammates left for Ridge Camp soon after camp was pitched. It rained steadily.

Lou, Jim, and I watched as the Indians, oblivious to the danger overhead, crossed back slowly under the snout of the glacier. Just as they approached the far side, a small avalanche shot over the lip of the snout and wiped out their tracks, narrowly missing Surrendra.

"That's as close to Russian roulette as you can get," I remarked and crawled back into the tent.

Tomorrow was to be our first day of actual roped climbing on the face. The three of us enjoyed a beautiful red sunset and the hope of a clear dawn.

SIX

We were awake at 5:00 A.M. The clear sunset of the evening before had been deceptive. Snow and rain had fallen most of the night and thick, misty clouds surrounded us. The mountain was a world of white, a dramatic change from yesterday's earth tones of rust and brown.

Jim started breakfast in his two-man A-frame tent, while in our tent Lou and I maneuvered ourselves to opposite ends to dress. The roomier dome tents had not been developed yet, and even putting our boots on was a chore. We became lightheaded and breathless.

After a meager breakfast and a quick radio call to Willi, the three of us loaded our packs with rope and hardware and began the thousand-foot climb to the base of the rock buttress. Lou set an easy pace, following the gentle ramp systems and zigzagging to avoid the many steep rock walls.

"Look who's coming from behind!" Jim said suddenly.

It was Elliot, catching up at a quick pace.

"I wonder what came over him this morning?" I asked.

"Must be he's feeling guilty he's not up here with us," Jim explained. "It's pushed him beyond his good judgment."

He waved to Elliot and continued climbing.

The roping-up point was a steep change in the terrain. Preparing for the first roped pitch, we found a stance to put on crampons. The crumbling black schist offered no place for a piton, so I took a three-foot tubular picket and drove it into a two-inch-wide bottomless crack. The aluminum bent and mangled, welding perfectly to the rock.

"Since they're no good for the snow and ice, we may as well use them for rock," I remarked. The idea worked perfectly. Meanwhile, Elliot caught up with us.

"Elliot, you made it!" Lou said enthusiastically. "Want to lead the first pitch?"

"I don't feel right just yet," he replied. "An avalanche just about got me on the way over this morning . . . I thought everything I've been worried about was going to happen right there, but it missed me by a few feet."

"O.K.," Lou said. "Well . . . Jim, you go ahead and lead the first pitch."

Protected from avalanches by the rock cliffs above, Jim tied in and began traversing onto the glacier. He led a 150-foot pitch slanting right in the deep, slushy snow, and disappeared around several rock corners. Lou and I followed, removing any pitons or pickets Jim had placed during his lead. We also fixed the rope that Jim had for the team's use to carry loads up the mountain.

My turn was next. I led three more pitches, belaying under small overhangs and behind small rock steps to avoid the few rocks that were falling. A heavy drizzle continued to fall.

Lou led the last pitch. Blinded by what was now sleet and heavy fog, he traversed a forty-degree ice slope to an isolated rock outcrop on the main face. He tied off to a strong picket driven into a crack in the rock, then returned to my belay.

"The steady hiss over there is a continuous avalanche," Lou explained. "I should have gone straight up this ice slope instead of traversing to that outcrop. We'll have to fix it tomorrow."

We gained considerable height protected by the rock walls, but now the route would have to be pushed onto avalanche slopes above. Tired and soaked to the skin, our crampons balling up badly with snow, we rappeled back to the start of the ropes. In half an hour we were back at Advanced Base.

To our surprise, Devi's smiling face popped out of

Jim's tent door. She had crossed the glacier with Elliot while we were up pitching the lines. "Elliot and I just started dinner," she said happily. "How did the route look?"

"Good to where we got, Dev," Lou replied. "Are you and Elliot the only ones to move over today?"

"Yeah, it will be a little crowded until another tent is brought over," she apologized.

Although Jim looked a little forlorn at having to share his two-man tent with two other people, he realized this would be his first chance to enjoy Devi's company. Since our departure from New Delhi, Jim and Devi shared a sensitivity about climbing the mountain. For them, this was an emotional adventure as well as a physical challenge.

Radio call brought great news. Ad had made the trip to Ridge Camp after all. We thought surely this would convince him to stay.

"Are you coming over to Advanced Base, Ad?" Lou asked.

"I'll see how I feel," he answered. "I'm only going to be here several days, then I'll be going out to Lata."

"John's curious as to what happened to the mail . . . ?" Lou asked.

"It's supposed to be here," Ad replied. "I don't know what's happened to the mail runner."

Lou signed off. "My wife's eight months pregnant and I can't even find out how she's doing!" he moaned, exasperated.

"It's the same curse on every expedition," I remembered. "No mail until we're finished and on the way out. I remember when we left Dhaulagiri in seventy-three, I got a three-month-old letter from Joyce telling me she just bought a new house and moved in!"

"What I remember from Dhaulagiri," Lou chuckled, "was Watergate. It had come and gone and we never heard a thing about it until we got home."

We were all asleep early, so I woke up before dawn. I could hear small avalanches breaking loose along the mountainside; it was almost soothing, listening and knowing how far away they were. But one exploded loudly as it left the glacier's tongue.

"Grab the poles!" I screamed into the dark of the tent. "Avalanche!"

No sooner had I finished than the wind blast from an avalanche on the glacier several hundred yards away smacked the tents ferociously. It lasted for what seemed an eternity. Miraculously, the tent poles remained intact. Everyone was all right, although frightened. No one slept much the rest of the night.

Next morning at radio call we told the others at Ridge it was unsafe either to move up or attempt to cross to Advanced Base. Willi hedged, saying he would consider our advice until midmorning. Around 10:00 A.M. five porters and all the sahibs except Ad carried across the glacier and up to Advanced Base.

The stress of the bad weather and avalanche danger had put everyone on edge. On his way back from the latrine, Jim overheard Willi in his tent say to Andy, "States didn't take enough Freud in med school."

Jim knew the remark was in reference to his attempts to make Elliot comfortable with his decision to leave the expedition. He had counseled people for years as part of his medical practice and knew Elliot needed someone to talk with. To Jim, Willi's remark was just another in a long list attesting to Willi's belief that Jim didn't know what he was doing medically. I could see Jim was angry, but he went back to his tent without saying anything.

The second discussion of the day concerning the route began calmly, but tempers flared quickly. Jim, still fuming over Willi's remark an hour earlier, exploded.

"I've had it!" Jim yelled, turning toward Willi. "I'll give this place one week, then I'm leaving. This is wasting my time. There are other mountains to climb."

There was a pall over the group as we felt the sting of Jim's disgust. Even the mountain was finally still.

I broke the uneasy silence. "We have several alternatives. Let's talk them out."

There were three alternatives to the danger and bad weather we were encountering. The first was to wait for a week, to see if the weather improved and the danger subsided. This idea seemed rational but not ideal. Waiting is tough even for experienced Himalayan climbers. Andy and Elliot voiced opinions to go down and abandon the route, while Lou, Willi, and I agreed the waiting was reasonable.

"The second alternative," Lou began, "is to send a four-man alpine-style team of the strongest climbers for the summit."

Lou was thinking of himself, Jim, Peter, and me as candidates for the alpine push—and everyone knew it. I was for this style. It would be safer and we could break away from those on the team who didn't want to be there. The Indians weren't talking, but I had to assume they didn't favor this method.

No one discounted the idea. The avalanches had everyone scared.

"It's too early yet to think about that one," Willi mumbled.

"Third would be to abandon this route and climb elsewhere in the Sanctuary," Lou continued.

"You know we won't climb 'elsewhere,' " I said with contempt for the idea. "Once we abandon this route, we may as well go home. All our supplies are here and I, for one, don't care to climb anything else."

"I'm open to what the team wants," Devi added quietly. "We could still climb the standard route on the south."

Willi expressed a Himalayan climber's point of view best: "We've got to relax, take it easy, and wait it out."

I agreed with Willi and so did several of the others. Himalayan climbing is a game of patience. The mountain hurls everything it has at you, then waits to see if you'll quit. We just hadn't given it enough time to get better.

Jim was still too upset with Willi and wouldn't listen. Becoming almost violent, he again threatened to leave. He picked up his pack and left camp, intending to burn off his anger by retrieving gear that had been brought across the glacier and left several hundred yards below Advanced Base.

I felt a little embarrassed by Jim's outbreak, which to me indicated a deep resentment toward Willi as a leader.

The friction that had separated the team at Dibrugheta was still apparent on the mountain and showing itself because of the stress we were under.

I picked up my pack and caught Jim on his way down to the cache. We didn't talk much, but knowing the other cared was enough. We picked up ropes and food, then started back for camp. Willi, on his way back down to Ridge Camp, tried to smooth Jim's angry feelings, but had little success. Jim was in no mood to listen to Willi's explanations.

A four-man tent was set up for Jim, Devi, and Elliot, who could now spread out and retain some privacy. Devi began dinner soon after the tent was pitched. Lou and I discussed the possibilities of a four-man alpine ascent. The team wasn't looking very committed and every contingency had to be considered. Devi's yodel to dinner ended our meeting.

"John, you cook the biscuits," Devi requested. "I'll cook the meat, potatoes, and corn."

She involved me pleasantly in the dinner preparation. I enjoyed that. It became a challenge to try and cook the best unburned biscuits in camp. That night we didn't talk about Nanda Devi or our intended route. Jim, Lou, Devi, Elliot, and I shared a pleasant evening. Jim was back to his usual self and we all turned in shortly after dark.

Around 2:30 A.M. another big avalanche swept by, its wind slashing at our tents.

How terrifying an avalanche in the dark can be: the grating, rasping sounds—the blackness. Each avalanche seemed intent on roaring into camp and burying us alive—always at night. I would jerk into a sitting position, my eyes wide and searching, expecting to see it burst through the tent walls. I would strain desperately to hear where the cold death was heading, but the sound was deceiving and it was hard for me to tell where it was. My heart seemingly would stop along with my breathing. Then the blast of wind that is pushed ahead of large avalanches would hit the tent and the noise would shoot by. My breathing would return and my heart would pound as if it wanted out of my chest. We were completely at nature's mercy.

I may have been more conscious of being buried than the others, having experienced cold death in the night in Russia several years before. As we slept high on an unclimbed north face, a small slide buried our two tents. Only three of the four of us survived: the fourth climber was buried too deep for us to get to him in time. The thought of the moment kept me ever on edge during my nights on Nanda Devi.

It was 6:05 A.M., the first of August.

"Ridge, this is Advanced Base," I called over the radio. The weather had become worse, dumping several feet of powder snow in camp through the night.

Willi answered. "Read you, John. How do things look?"

"Pretty bad, Willi," I said. "We had another bad blast of wind last night and I feel there's going to be another one pretty soon. It would be best if no one came over today."

"Well, we'll think about it over here," Willi remarked. "You guys have said that before."

"No, Willi, I'm serious. It looks really bad."

My instinct was right. I heard the avalanche coming several minutes later. "Big Daddy" had started high on the Northwest Face, swelling as it tumbled down the glacier. After falling eight thousand feet, it was a giant.

"Hear that, Lou?" We held our breath, staring at each other inside the tent. "Hold the tent poles!" I yelled. I grabbed the front two as Lou started for the rear.

He was too late. The blast of wind and snow hit the camp like an explosion and the poles snapped. Our tent door was half open and I struggled to watch the frightening scene unfolding at the four-man tent several yards away.

Devi, Jim, and Elliot hadn't heard the blast coming. Both Devi and Elliot were coming back from the toilet in their long johns when the wind hit. Jim, pouring Roman Meal cereal into a pot of boiling water, was sitting in the open door of the tent.

Within seconds the blast of snow had ripped the heavy nylon from the aluminum frame, sending Jim, the Roman Meal, and the tent spinning fifteen feet toward the cliff a short distance away. Screaming, Elliot barely managed to jump on the tent and stop the whole mess from going into the gorge. The blast lasted for several minutes. Packs, boxes of dehydrated food, and tent parts disappeared over the cliff to settle hundreds of feet below.

Lou and I dressed and began helping the others find warm clothes. Both Elliot and Devi were all but frozen. Snow clung to their hair and underwear.

"Here's my coat, Devi. Get this on."

"Where's Jim?"

"He's still in the tent!"

"Help me find the door!" Jim yelled from inside the collapsed tent. The flap popped open to reveal Jim, covered with Roman Meal from head to foot, grinning madly and still holding the now empty pot.

"Anyone for oatmeal?" Jim asked wryly.

Our well-ordered camp was destroyed. The poles of all three tents had snapped like kindling. The four-man tent had taken the worst beating—all of the heavy-gauge aluminum 3/4-inch poles bent to some degree. The two 1 1/2-inch top poles had snapped in half at the connecting holes. Both two-man tents had broken poles, although we had salvaged several by holding them during the blast.

Elliot, Devi, and Jim, frozen from the snow and wind, gathered their warm clothing and sleeping bags out of the wrecked tent and sought warmth in the extra two-man. Lou and I began removing the broken tent poles and replacing them with spares. Within an hour, a warm breakfast had been prepared for the three "homeless" and camp was again in one piece.

Elliot, Jim, and Devi chattered away for hours to relieve their strung-out nerves. The mountain was showing its teeth and Elliot was becoming more certain he didn't want to be there. Meanwhile, Lou and I began searching for the missing gear that had blown over the ridge crest.

"You know what's missing, don't you, John?" Lou cried. "The three cans of freeze-dried ice cream! The only ice cream we have!"

The loss was great, indeed. Lou, full of energy, descended hundreds of feet over the side of the ridge looking for Elliot's pack and the food. I searched the rock

Ad Carter

John Evans

Elliot Fisher

Andy Harvard

Marty Hoey

Peter Lev

Lou Reichardt

John Roskelley

Jim States

Nanda Devi Unsoeld

Willi Unsoeld

New Delhi preparations. Left to right: *Devi, Elliot, Andy, Marty, Willi.*

Left to right: *Ad, Devi, Jagatsingh, Willi*

Nirmal carrying Marty to Dibrugheta

Base Camp in the Sanctuary

Devi, Andy, porters, and the meat from a sacrificed goat

The author during the approach

Jim at Advanced Base

Advanced Base Camp

Advanced Base Camp

Ridge Camp

Jim cooking at Advanced Base Camp

Setting up Camp I

Camp I

Jim approaching Camp I

Above Camp I

Camp II after a storm

Lou and Jim approach the Buttress from Camp III

Lou and Jim on top

The Northwest Face of Nanda Devi

The difficult North Buttress and summit of Nanda Devi

Devi

NANDA DEVI
25,645
"Sugar Delight"
Snowfield
24,000
IV
North Buttress
22,800
III
North Ridge
Southwest Ridge
1936
Route
19,900
II
19,100
I
Steep snow
and ice
17,100
Advance Base
17,000
Ridge Camp
Ice cliff
cone
To Base Camp
13,500
©D. Molenaar
NANDA DEVI
25,645
Nanda Devi
From West

crevices just below the cliff. The others were still in their tent.

"I found one!" Lou's voice floated up over the ridge. He slowly made his way back to camp. "It's vanilla," he said, holding up his prize.

Another avalanche blast, smaller than the last, rumbled through camp. It left a fine layer of powder on the entire ridge. The deep green and yellow moss hiding under small overhangs along the cliff seemed out of its element in our frozen white world.

"This is a bad time to be climbing Nanda Devi, Lou," I said.

"Well, this was the only time of year Ad could get off from teaching school. Monsoon or no monsoon, we're here now," he replied.

As the fog lifted, we could see Ridge Camp below had been placed well out of touch by avalanches. We heard Willi cut loose with his familiar yodel, a signal for us to turn on the radio. He had wisely decided not to chance a crossing under the glacier.

Back in our tent, Lou and I opened the can of vanilla ice cream.

"Say, did you guys find anything?" Jim called from the other tent a few feet away.

"Not everything," Lou said, swallowing his laughter between bites of vanilla. "Couldn't find the ice cream, but I got Elliot's pack."

Lou and I laughed silently while enjoying the ice cream. We planned to surprise the others after we had devoured our hard-earned share. Suddenly, Jim appeared at our door and peeked in. We burst into laughter and handed him some ice cream.

"I knew it was too quiet over here," Jim kidded.

Lou bagged some for Devi and Elliot and handed it to them, too. They were delighted with the unexpected treat. The five of us feasted on vanilla ice cream the rest of the afternoon

SEVEN

At 2:00 P.M. radio call, Willi told us all the sahibs at Ridge would be moving over to join us at Advanced Base the next day. "That's fine, Willi," I said, "but leave Surrendra at Ridge. Everytime he moves into camp to cook, I get the shits!"

"It's all psychological, John," Willi laughed. "Wait . . . Ad wants to say something to all of you."

Ad's voice came over the radio thinly. "I'm going back to Base tomorrow and within the next few days I'll be leaving for New Delhi. You're doing a great job and I don't feel needed anymore. My job was organization and that's completed."

"Ad," Lou began, "we understand what you're saying, but we still need you. We sure could use you at Base and Ridge camps for the next several weeks to shuttle the right food and gear up to us on the mountain."

"I'll do what I can in the next few days and leave with the outgoing mail runners if they ever get here," Ad replied.

"Please stay, Ad," Devi pleaded. "You should be here when we climb to the summit. It's your expedition more than anyone else's."

"Ann would want you to stay, Ad," Lou continued. "You could run the logistics from Base while Willi and I made the decisions on the mountain."

"Ad, this is Jim. We want you to know we care about you—whatever decision you make."

Willi came on the radio several times during the discussion endorsing Ad's decision. It was as though Willi finally knew that the expedition couldn't survive with two leaders.

Despite all the protests and words of encouragement to stay, Ad's mind was made up.

"Give me that radio, Lou," I demanded. "Ad, you can't leave the expedition just like that! You came in with intentions of carrying and helping on the mountain as high as you could go. I asked you several times in the States to add another strong climber, but you said no because in your opinion the team was strong enough. With Marty gone and John Evans not here, your leaving could mean the difference between success or failure. None of us feel like being here in these conditions either, but we're going to give it all we have."

"Well, I appreciate your wanting me to stay, John," he replied. "That's good of you. I liked being with everyone and wish all of you all the luck in the world. I know you can do it. Of course, I'll be in touch for several more days from Base. Over and out."

The five of us at Advanced Base stared at each other in disbelief. "I don't believe he heard me!" I said. Everyone except Ad had gotten my point.

Ad's decision to leave in the middle of the expedition discouraged most of us. Only Willi condoned his departure openly because he wanted the team to stick it out and the expedition to continue without any ill effects.

Lou was also sensitive to the issue. In a letter to his wife he wrote, "I feel particularly irritated because Ad determined what we would eat and climb with and the timing of this trip has been arranged for his convenience. I feel he has a responsibility he can't dump onto me as climbing leader."

But the issue was dropped. Ad was leaving and that was that. We would regroup and go on.

That afternoon I started work rebending the four-man-tent poles, while Lou worked on whittling wood plugs to fix the two-man-tent poles. By midafternoon, Roskelley & Reichardt Metal Refabricators, Inc. had fixed and put the broken poles back into place. The day came to an end with a promise of clear weather to come. We needed the hope.

* * *

The morning of August 2 was magnificent. Anxious to get started, we were up at 6:00 A.M. flipping pancakes. With loads heavier than usual because of the wet ropes, we slowly gained height to the fixed lines. The lines, unused for several days, were buried deep; it took over an hour for the first man to break trail and free the icy ropes.

Lou retrieved his last roped lead from the outcrop and led out another three hundred feet on fifty-degree ice to a sheltered rock stance on a rib away from avalanche danger. I untangled another rat's nest of nine-millimeter rope and led straight up over snow-covered rock to another tiny stance fifty feet below a large overhanging wall. After tying off the rope to an ice screw driven in the crumbling rock, I dragged a loose eight-millimeter rope to the wall and fastened it securely.

Soon Lou appeared, struggling in the deep wet snow of midday. A few steps at a time he moved closer, but slowly, not yet acclimatized to 19,000 feet. I hid under the roof of the overhang, trying to avoid the sun's heat and the constant drip of water off the wall's lip.

"Welcome to Camp I, Lou," I said enthusiastically.

"This isn't as high as I would have liked to put Camp I, but otherwise it's perfect," he answered. "I'll head out around the corner one more pitch to have a look."

The rope payed out slowly until finally it stopped altogether. He drove a picket, tied the rope off, and descended to the overhang.

That day the sun became our enemy. It was too hot to push farther and the snow was slushy and knee deep. First Jim, then Devi, appeared just below us and laboriously made their way to the cave.

"Say, I've got the crackers and jerky," Devi said. "Everyone throw in what they have and let's eat."

We passed the tidbits of food while enjoying the beautiful scene of mountains rising before us. After a brief siesta, we descended to Advanced Base, making the eight three-hundred-foot rappels in less than half an hour. By 2:00 P.M. we were all back at Advanced Base.

Camp had become a small village in the few hours we

were gone. Peter, Andy, Nirmal, and Kiran were already there, having moved up from Ridge Camp. Jim and I saw the need for a latrine and descended over the cliff a few feet to build one complete with a flagstone seat. The work of art became known as "le John," not only because I had helped build it, but because, as I was later told, it also had a "cold and heartless personality."

Jim left camp alone early the next morning to ascend the fixed lines. Peter, his appointed partner, decided to stay in camp after he woke up feeling ill.

"Andy, why don't you lead with Jim today?" Lou asked. "You better get started."

"I've got diarrhea real bad," Andy complained. "I'm in no shape to go either."

"What about you, Devi?" Lou asked.

"I'd rather carry later when I'm feeling better," she replied. Devi had been suffering from periodic bouts of diarrhea and a cough she had picked up in Nepal before the trip. She wouldn't talk about her hernia. Although ill at times, Devi would push herself to perform above the standards of some of the healthier sahibs.

Although I was supposed to be support only for the three chosen lead climbers, I was ready and left camp immediately to catch Jim. We were soon to the end of the fixed lines above Camp I.

I led another three-hundred-foot pitch, placing rock pins for protection on several outcrops along the snow slope we were ascending. The angle of the snow increased to fifty degrees as I ended the pitch. Jim arrived, dragging another three-hundred-foot rope. Having sat and rested while Jim worked, I volunteered to lead again.

A short ice-shoot to a wall went quickly. I then traversed onto a large snow slope and ran out of rope alongside a rock tower standing alone in the center of the snowfield.

The heat became almost unbearable. We were sweating profusely and breathing with difficulty. It was like running a marathon with a pillow over my face. The extra loads of rope we were carrying now became a burden. Lou appeared a short distance below and was soon at our small but safe stance. I again led straight up to reach a short 5-

foot rock wall 150 feet above. A bombproof picket driven into the wall secured the rope.

"The snow's really bad," I called to the others. "It could avalanche!" Jim and Lou agreed, so we rappeled back to Camp I.

"Devi! How are you feeling?" I said as we entered camp.

"A lot better," she said. "Good enough to carry to here, anyway."

Nirmal and Kiran had also carried and were resting beneath the shade of the overhang. They were acclimatizing well, better than most of the Americans. We needed their strength.

It was still early in the afternoon, so the two groups each began to build a future tent platform. The soil under the snow was frozen and difficult to excavate. We pushed, lifted, and pulled to roll huge boulders onto the slope below. Eventually two respectable sites took shape. Exhausted, we decided to descend and work on them again the next day.

Nirmal hand-lined down to the first difficult rappel and began setting up his brake system. I followed closely, eager to get started.

"Hold on, Nirmal," I said, glancing at his carabiner-brake rappel system. "Those two middle carabiners are upside down. They need their backs to the rope."

He acknowledged my help, fixed his system, then descended. I again landed next to him after a few minutes' delay.

"Nirmal, you're doing the same thing again!" I scolded, repeating my previous instructions. "Flip those carabiners!"

From then on I watched Nirmal closely. His mistakes could have cost him his life. Kiran descended by hand-lining down the ropes without hooking onto them with a carabiner at all. By the time I reached the bottom of the ropes, I was convinced our Indian companions were not as careful or experienced as I had first believed.

That afternoon, Willi and the six high-altitude porters moved to Advanced Base. The camp became unusually noisy between discussions about the route and Kiran constantly yelling from his tent for Jatendra to wait on him. The caste system was evident even here. Jim was particularly annoyed at this display. He detested the master-and-servant customs that Kiran took for granted even on the mountain. More than once Jim argued with Kiran openly on the subject.

The weather looked bad as the night's cold drove us into our sleeping bags. But sleeping was out of the question. Throughout the night I woke to the sound of rain and snow on the tent roof.

A curtain of rain greeted us on the morning of August 4. It was obvious we weren't going to be climbing. There was just too much snow. Lou and I, then Jim, Kiran, and several porters crossed back to Ridge Camp for the remainder of the gear still there.

Several hundred yards below camp we came upon two loads that had been dropped, broken open, and left uncovered. Much of their contents, including most of our precious matches, were destroyed by the heavy rains.

"Whichever porter did this is going to get his ass kicked off this mountain, Lou!" I yelled. "This is complete waste!"

Lou stood shaking his head in disbelief.

In my anger, I raced ahead across the glacier, picked up the fifty pounds of oxygen, and started back for Advanced Base. Jim was forced to listen to my raving, as was poor Kiran and Jatendra, who caught the brunt of my vicious mood.

"Kiran! When you get back to camp, I want you to find out which porters dumped that gear and left it to ruin in the rain!" I shouted.

He yelled back from up the hill. "No problem, I will take care of it."

My mood became uglier when I realized that most of the gear that was supposed to have been brought up to Advanced Base was still at the cache below camp. The porters had not been supervised properly. This would have to be corrected.

Once at camp, I saw the porters huddling in their tent. I ordered them into the rain to descend and pick up all the loads below camp, including those that had been broken open. They sensed my ill temper and departed immediately.

Willi apologized for the broken loads and tried to explain why the loads had been left down below when the porters should have brought them up. Lou didn't agree with Willi. He felt the job had been neglected.

Devi interrupted their argument. "This won't solve what has already happened," she reasoned. "Let's learn from it, but not create any more bad feelings."

She was right, and Lou and Willi dropped the issue.

Later, at dinner, Elliot announced his decision to leave the expedition. "I have no desire to be here," he admitted, "but feel I have an obligation to stay."

Elliot was torn. One minute he was laughing and joking and talking, only to become sullen, quiet, and unresponsive the next. He didn't want to be there, but felt enormous guilt for even thinking of leaving. It happens to all of us sooner or later: your sixth sense says to leave, to save yourself, but obligation tells you that you must follow through on your commitment.

"Only John and Jim are indispensable, Elliot," Lou consoled him. "Obligations shouldn't keep you from being true to yourself."

Elliot took that as his pass to leave. "I'll supervise the ferrying of loads from Ridge before I go," he offered. It was a problem Lou was glad to have solved.

The other team members were relieved that Elliot had finally made his decision to leave. No one wanted to see him torture himself any longer, and his indecision was definitely detrimental to others whose commitment to the climb was wavering.

We would now be down to nine members from the original team of thirteen. With several climbers more or less constantly ill, we were essentially half a team.

Surrendra had moved over with Willi from Ridge that morning to cook. My first blast of diarrhea since I had left him at Ridge was an appropriate ending to a dreary day.

The next morning it was still snowing and turning to a cold sleet. Heavy dark clouds enveloped the camp; they lifted occasionally to reveal a fresh layer of snow on all the surrounding peaks. Small avalanches roared by in the mist, but the big one we were waiting for didn't occur. The thought of what was compounding above was scary enough to keep us awake at night. It was another rest day.

Living conditions had degenerated badly. I found myself nearly floating in water that had leaked into the floor of the tent. Every day we had to sponge it out, cleaning up as much dirt as we could in the process.

Most of the team had books to rely on when confined to camp. The titles in our library included *Moby Dick*, *All the President's Men*, *Demian* and *The Journey to the East* by Hesse, *The Owl's Song*, and *Tinker, Tailor, Soldier, Spy* by le Carre. Devi contributed *Chinga Shakes the World* by Jack Belden; Ad once offered Dickens's *Oliver Twist*. When we tired of books, visits to the other tents for discussions of home occupied our time. Patience was the most valued virtue. Few had it this late in the expedition.

Devi sorted food for our meals during the day and discovered a large tin of cookies. With these in hand, she visited each tent. Later, we were treated to a cake she made from odds and ends. Devi made the camp more pleasant on snow days; her presence made us all act a little more civilized even under those conditions.

Jim concerned himself with Elliot and making him feel his decision to leave was the right one. Elliot had not decided when he was going because he still felt he was letting the team down.

I could appreciate Elliot's decision. He lacked confidence in himself and was plagued by a feeling of impending doom on the mountain. He was also worried about school and his girlfriend back home. But I couldn't openly condone his decision to leave. Many excellent climbers truly committed to the sport had applied for this expedition. They would have given anything to climb Nanda Devi. Yet they were refused because, according to Carter, "We already have a strong team."

That evening after dinner we discussed the team's performance. Lou was critical of several members because they kept moving to higher camps with illnesses.

Although they were repeatedly asked to descend to clear up their coughs or diarrhea, they would not. This reluctance to descend not only endangered the rest of the team's health, but also used valuable food supplies without advancing the route.

Lou made the situation clear. "Everyone that isn't carrying should descend to Base to take care of his or her problem. No one is going to get better by going higher."

Jim elaborated. "We have to be extremely aware of sudden changes in each other's looks, feelings, or personalities as we go higher," he said. "Pulmonary edema, cerebral edema, and high altitude sickness can occur too quickly and many times the victim becomes unconscious before we can diagnose it." He continued to explain the symptoms and treatment for each problem that was common to high-altitude exposure.

Willi then briefly explained how to connect the regulators to the oxygen cylinders we had brought for illness and what oxygen flow to give the victim. The oxygen would not be used for climbing. By the time he was done it was late, and we all left to search for our own tents. It was still raining hard.

The next morning the sky seemed to be clearing. I dressed and walked up to the cook tarp where Surrendra and Jatendra were busy making tea and oatmeal. I found a metal cup and filled it with sweet tea, more to warm my hands than to drink.

Surrendra was an expert at starting a fire even with the wet wood that had been lying in the rain and snow for days. He would squat for hours in front of the fire, bending over to blow at the coals to keep a spark alive. Jatendra would relieve him when needed.

I could hear the other porters talking in their four-man tent a few feet away. Their laughter broke the calm of the early morning.

"Sahib," Surrendra caught my attention. "Go?" He pointed into the thick gray clouds.

"No, Surrendra," I said, indicating too much rain. I filled my bowl with mush and ate in the cook tarp while Jatendra served the other sahibs in their tents.

After breakfast, most of the team came out to survey the clearing sky. Conversation centered on those who were still sick but would not descend. There was anger in everyone's voice. The bad weather and resulting boredom had finally sapped our morale. I couldn't take any more of the petty disagreements.

"I'm going down to Base Camp," I announced. "I have a hunch the mail's coming today and I want to be there when it does. Anybody want to go?" My effort to get several of the sick members to descend fizzled. I was all alone with my decision.

I threw a few items of clothing into my pack and said good-bye. Despite the long journey to Base, I was glad to be alone. I felt better emotionally than I had for days.

At the glacier's edge, I started running to avoid any avalanche that may have cut loose. The effort of running at 17,000 feet with a load gave me a deep cough that would stay with me for several weeks. I scurried up to Ridge Camp, waved to Advanced Base, and dropped the thirty-five-hundred feet down the gully in less than an hour. At the Rishi, the natural snow bridge and avalanche debris had grown to frightening proportions. Gigantic blocks of ice, snow, and rock made me detour some distance before I felt safe crossing the river. Once on the other side, off the mountain, I was able to relax.

"Hello Ad!" I greeted him outside his tent.

"John! What are you doing here?"

"Just came to get the mail," I replied. "I have a hunch it's coming today."

Ad cooked some soup and tea while I searched through the equipment boxes for gear to send to Advanced Base. There were many items at Base that we needed on the mountain, so I packed them into a porter load to be sent up.

Ad and I spent the remainder of the afternoon talking about his family. We both avoided the ticklish issue of his leaving the mountain.

"Here comes a porter! It's Dharamsingh."

I was out of the tent in an instant and rushed to meet him. Smiling, he greeted me at the stream. He looked refreshed even though he had just covered the trek from

Lata in two days. Close behind were two other porters loaded with fresh vegetables, and their dog. One of the porters, Ballsingh, had brought a British flintlock rifle to hunt the wild sheep in the Sanctuary and, after dropping his load, set out after the elusive animals.

"Mail, Dharamsingh?" I asked anxiously.

"Ah, yes, Sahib," he grinned and handed over the long-awaited news from home, a small packet containing five letters.

"This is all?" I asked.

Thumbing through the letters, my excitement faded. Only Kiran, Nirmal, and Surrendra had received any mail.

"What the hell happened, Ad?" I asked. "This is your department."

"I don't know," he said, disturbed. "It must have gotten fouled up at the embassy in New Delhi."

It was an obvious error in the mailing address. We relayed the bad news to the others on the 7:00 P.M. radio call. Everyone was disappointed. With morale already sagging, this incident just added to the general depression.

"Lou, if the weather is still bad tomorrow, I may run out to Joshimath and see what the foul-up is with the mail," I said. "It would only take four days at the most, in and out, and it would make a big difference to all of us at this point."

"I wish you wouldn't," Lou pleaded, "but I can't stop you."

Dharamsingh then relayed information to Kiran over the radio for almost twenty minutes. Something was amiss.

Kiran told Ad the news. "According to Dharamsingh, one of the porters stripped the gorge of fixed line on his way out. We may have some trouble getting all the porters to carry without it when we need to leave the mountain. Anyway, I've told Dharamsingh to notify the police in Joshimath when he goes out. Ad, when you get there, you must also complain."

The radio call ended after Lou told Ad to wait for Elliot. He had decided to depart with Ad. In the meantime, we had no idea where John Evans was. He was needed not only for his strength, but also for emotional support. I began to refer to Evans as "the Messiah."

The weather was clear and cold on August 7. Willi, Jim, and Peter packed and moved to Camp I so they could push the route higher during the next few days. The other sahibs carried loads, then descended to Advanced Base.

After a short but emotional send-off that morning, Elliot crossed over to Ridge Camp with the porters and supervised the transport of the rest of the loads to Advanced Base. Because of the unexpected good weather, I decided to return to camp to help carry loads. The mail would have to wait.

"Call my wife when you get home and tell her I love her, Ad," I said, and shook his hand.

"You'll do all right on the route," he said, staring toward the summit. "That buttress leans back from this angle."

"Yeah, well, we'll see." I started off after the two porters who were carrying sugar, fresh vegetables, matches, and the odds and ends I had found at Base.

Ad was excited to be leaving. Four porters and eventually the two that were carrying for me to Advanced Base were accompanying him and Elliot to Lata. Ad was packed and moving along the trail before I was at the Rishi snow bridge. As I watched him disappear down the gorge, I couldn't help but feel intense loneliness and despair. I turned into the gully and began the long climb to Advanced Base.

Halfway to Ridge Camp, Elliot and I met for the last time.

"Damn it, Elliot," I said, "I wish you hadn't made this decision . . . but at least you made one. I hope you know what you're doing."

"I'm sorry. But I have to do this for me," he replied. We both sat looking into the dirt, tears welling up in our eyes.

"You know, I'd like to go out too, Elliot. All of us would. This mountain's dangerous and someone's going to be killed."

"If that's what you believe, then why don't you leave and get off the mountain?"

"Because it's not going to be me," I replied.

We looked at each other.

"Do you want me to do anything for you when I get out?" he offered.

"Yeah. Call my wife. Tell her I'm fine and to send me a pair of large tennis shoes, size 11½. Mine have had it," I said.

We parted. I watched him descend a way. I proceeded to Ridge Camp.

The two porters and their wirehaired mutt were waiting for me to arrive. It was still early afternoon, so I offered them five extra rupees to carry to camp. They jumped at my offer. As it turned out, they had intended to go across to Advanced Base anyway to see their relative, one of our porters.

Finding two ice axes at the cache, I gave each of them one and led them across the glacier and up to camp. The dog followed, acting as if this were a normal day in the life of a Garhwali canine.

"John! Good to see you," Lou yelled as I entered Advanced Base. "Who's your friend?"

"Oh, that's Ballsingh's dog. He and another porter are just behind carrying all the goodies."

"Hi John," Devi said, poking her head out of the tent. "Glad you're back. We were worried you had gone out."

"I feel a lot better now that I'm back with you," I admitted.

The two porters arrived, helped by our men who were happy to hear news from the village. They all disappeared into their tent to listen to the new visitors.

Dinner was an extra treat of baked apples, cooked cabbage, onions, and freeze-dried meat. Dharamsingh had known we would be hungry for fresh food.

We assessed our situation. With the porters' help, the logistical supplies could build quickly at each camp. Our success depended entirely on the weather, which to this point had suppressed our efforts easily. A few good days would push the route higher and strengthen our morale.

That afternoon Nirmal strung a rope through camp to

simulate a fixed line. The basic mountaineering school for the porters had begun. With our help, Nirmal taught our high-altitude porters to use Gibbs ascenders, a mechanical device for going up the ropes safely. Each time one reached the top of the line, one of us would show him how to set up a rappel and go back down. Fast and enthusiastic learners, they were "experts" before dark in ascending and descending the ropes.

The team was alive once more, although Elliot and Ad were gone. An amputation had taken place, but as a team we had survived.

EIGHT

I was in a hurry to leave ahead of the six porters and the other sahibs carrying to Camp I. The porters would undoubtedly be slow on the ropes and I didn't want to freeze while waiting for them.

It was 5:30 A.M. "Ready to go?" I asked Lou.

"Go ahead, I'll catch you in a few minutes."

The ropes were buried deep under the fresh snow and our loads were heavy. Lou and I arrived at an empty Camp I by 8:30. We unloaded all but one rope each and continued up the fresh tracks above camp. Jim was nowhere to be seen. Willi was a short lead past our previous high point; Peter was poised at the base of a large cliff about four hundred feet above Willi. They were stopped and the problem was obvious at a glance.

Six hundred feet of line stretched between Peter and Willi and continued even farther down the slope. Tied to the end of this line were four coiled three-hundred-foot, nine-millimeter ropes. Peter was trying to haul the ropes from his small stance and Willi was straining hard to help. Communication between the two was difficult because of the distance; the load had ceased to budge. Hauling the ropes through the deep wet snow, rather than carrying them, just hadn't worked.

Willi, Peter, and Jim had discussed this system of hauling the previous day. Jim had argued against it but was outvoted. Earlier in the trip, Lou and I had both asked Peter not to try hauling, but he was determined.

Lou jumared to Peter, while I untangled the rat's nest of rope at Willi's belay station. Willi descended to the clump of four ropes and hooked them to his harness. He slowly made his way to me in an incredible display of determination. His stamina was astounding for an almost-fifty-year-old man. No wonder he had climbed Everest and Masherbrum.

With the belay point tied off and untangled, I grabbed a rope from Willi and jumared to the cliff while Lou and Peter argued over the merits of hauling.

"John! I'm over here!"

Jim appeared on my left. He sat on a cone of snow under a small overhang. It looked like an exposed but safe position.

"What the hell's Peter doing?" I asked. "Hauling is crazy on this low an angle of slope."

"I tried to convince Willi and Peter of that, but it was useless."

Lou finally sorted out the mess of ropes at Peter's stance and belayed him along a traverse to the cliff's corner to see the upper slopes for the next day. Peter was out of sight for some time and then we saw him rappel back to the traverse.

"It's long avalanche slope above and I couldn't get any good pins in," he said. "I finally managed to drive four in at one point."

"Never mind, Peter," I said. "Look, if there had been an easier way to carry loads up a mountain, someone would have thought of it by now. Hauling is not an answer to saving energy or time."

"All right, goddamn it! Drop it! I won't try it again."

One by one we descended to Camp I in the exhausting midday heat. We were greeted with good news. All six of the porters had carried to Camp I easily and had already descended. Kiran, Nirmal, and Devi were still at camp; only Andy had rested at Advanced Base because of his lingering cough.

Kiran, Nirmal, Lou, and I continued descending to Advanced Base, leaving Willi, Peter, and Jim to push the route farther the next day. On the way down, Lou and I discussed Peter's outburst and our insensitivity.

"We better lay off him," I said. "You can draw more flies with honey than with vinegar."

"Yeah, they felt pretty bad about losing so much time. I thought Willi was going to break his back trying to correct the whole mess."

"Let's stick to praise tomorrow no matter what happens. Jim's doing everything he can to add to their group and you *know* he's not exactly wanted up there."

The team was still split over Marty's incident at Dibrugheta, and by now, distinct "A" and "B" teams had emerged. The "B" team—as they called themselves—consisted of Andy, Devi, Elliot, Peter, and Willi. They called Jim, Lou, and me the "A" team. There were definitely bad feelings between the two groups, especially during discussions of the route and team movement up the mountain. Those in the B team were concerned that Jim, Lou, and I were setting ourselves up to acclimatize faster and reach the summit first. Technically, we could "fix" the route faster and illness had hampered the others' acclimatization. We were the natural picks to be in front because of our strength and health.

The problem of team unrest is a common one in Himalayan climbing. Carrying loads is like working on a pit crew for a Formula I race car. The pit crew does a lot of the labor but receives little of the glory. The lead climbers are the drivers—getting the action and the credit. In our case, though, not only did we have to lead, but we had to carry huge loads of rope and hardware to use while leading. Strong leadership would have prevented the animosities between the members of our team, but Lou did not have the others' respect and Willi led by example rather than by decision making.

Advanced Base was cold and covered in mist the next morning. Snow continued to fall since the previous afternoon and had turned to rain.

"My throat's real sore," I complained. "Are you going to carry today, Lou?"

"Yeah, just to Camp I, though," he said, putting on his boots.

"Oh hell, maybe I'll go anyway."

We loaded our packs and trudged through the fresh snow to the first of the fixed lines. The weather cleared for a short spell as we arrived at Camp I, dumped our loads of rope and food, and descended. We passed Nirmal, Kiran, and three porters carrying up. Lou was delighted with the stockpiling of supplies at Camp I since the porters had started carrying. We were almost ahead of ourselves.

Back at Advanced Base, I immediately went to bed after taking heavy doses of penicillin; my throat had worsened since morning. Devi and Andy had been bedridden with similar sore throats and coughs throughout the day. We all seemed to be living on pills: pills for colds, pills for sore throats, pills for diarrhea, vitamin pills, water purification pills. At times I thought we didn't need to eat.

Later that night Willi radioed in good news. Their day had gone well despite the bad weather. "We got another six hundred feet on really difficult ground up the left side of the snowfield," he said.

Peter suddenly broke in. "Willi did some fantastic leading over mixed ground. We're moving real well now!"

"Sounds great, guys," Lou replied. "Do it again tomorrow. How does it look from your high point?"

Willi said it looked difficult, but they would manage.

Jim, Willi, and Peter were awake and moving up the ropes at 3:00 A.M. the next morning. They were all feeling sluggish and exhausted. Jim was concerned about the deep loose snow, but given the choice to return to camp, he refused.

Jim reached a high point on the open slope and he continued leading. Another three hundred feet brought him to a five-foot rock wall and protection from avalanches. The two pitches up the open snowslope were always referred to from then on as "Jim's Lead."

Around 5:00 A.M. a strange, almost supernatural experience happened to Jim. He was overwhelmed by a disheartening premonition that his father had died. A cold sweat swept over him. Jim had experienced such feelings back home twice before and both times his father had been seriously ill. But now there was nothing he could do except keep climbing.

I later listened to Jim intently, hoping this one was just the hard work and heat of the day. The premonition was unnerving, especially since he had another about Lou getting hit by an avalanche down below. Lou had narrowly escaped one several days later. I gave Jim as much reassurance as I could, then quickly changed the subject.

That day the three established "Cache Ledge," which would later become the unplanned site for Camp II. It was an "eagle's perch" placed under a thirty-foot wall and well protected from rockfall and avalanche.

Peter pointed across a large gully to some protected cliffs. "I'm going to set up an alternate rappel route over there. It may save us during retreat in a bad snowstorm."

"The traverse across that gully is worse than rappeling from here!" Jim argued. "We can't afford to waste the rope and hardware for that."

Peter insisted. He needed to show the team that he was competent and that he deserved to be up front. Jim was too tired to argue further and watched as Willi set up a belay and Peter edged onto the slope.

He managed to traverse the gully with great difficulty, fighting the tangles and drag of the three-hundred-foot rope. Once across, he slipped and nearly swung over to Willi, two hundred feet away. Several hours later he finished fixing an alternate "safety" route that almost cost him his life.

That same morning Lou left Advanced Base early with a heavy load that he dumped at Cache Ledge. He traversed around the rock wall to watch the three lead climbers work. Their progress was disappointing. Less than four hundred feet had been fixed that day over easy ground. He descended to Advanced Base, passing hard-working Kiran and two of the stronger porters, Jatendra and Balbirsingh.

Willi made the 2:00 P.M. radio call to Lou.

"I checked your progress today and was pretty disappointed," Lou began. "I'm going to send John up tomorrow to give you a hand. He and Jim will be in support."

Willi wasn't pleased by this last bit of news. He had

hoped that Peter and he could make it to the North Ridge without anyone interfering.

"O.K.," Willi said, sounding glum, "we'll hit it hard tomorrow."

I had stayed in bed for the day pumping thousands of milligrams of Robicillin to kill my infection. My sore throat and crackling ears felt better. I was eager to move to Camp I and join Jim, who sounded depressed over the radio. He hadn't agreed with Peter's and Willi's decisions, considering many of them unsafe. Lou was sending me up to bolster Jim's morale as well as to help carry loads for Willi and Peter.

Willi announced a new development on the 7:00 P.M. radio call. "Peter and I are going to move up to Cache Ledge tomorrow and establish a camp there. Peter thinks that's a great place for Camp II and it will be a faster start for fixing pitches above."

"That's only eight hundred feet above Camp I!" Lou cried. "It's not spaced far enough to justify placing a camp!"

"Well, we think there isn't another spot for some distance yet, so this will give us an earlier start to get to the North Ridge," Willi insisted.

"But it will cost us a day's work on the route above!"

"Peter and I will move up in the morning and try and work on the route tomorrow afternoon," Willi replied.

"I didn't plan for tents, equipment, or food to be used between Camp I and the Main Ridge. We can't afford it logistically."

"It's the only way to reach the Ridge at this stage of the expedition."

Lou and I felt this was unnecessary, but neither Willi nor Peter were very fast climbers. Moving them higher would get more work accomplished on the route, despite using up a few loads of tents and camp gear.

"O.K.," Lou said, "but only until a camp is established on the North Ridge."

The weather was holding steady and August 11 was clear and windless: a perfect day. I packed my personal gear and left for Camp I early in hopes of avoiding the stifling heat. Lou chose to stay in camp to organize his own equipment, dry it out, and sort the last remaining loads that would go to Camp I.

Willi, Jim, and Peter remained at Camp I to sleep in and relax after their days of early-morning starts. I arrived in the heat, my sore throat having returned from the heavy breathing at 19,000 feet.

Jim invited me to share his tent as I dropped my load and greeted everyone. As often happens on a great day, the three men were feeling guilty for not using the day to fix lines. Willi was particularly disturbed by not pushing ahead. Willi and Peter came over to discuss the snow conditions with us.

"I think they're pretty bad, Peter," I said. "On the way up I dug into the slope and found a large layer of depth hoar." Metamorphosed by age and layering, these ice crystals form a breaking surface for avalanches.

Peter checked the snow himself on a slope outside camp. He dug deep through the layers of fresh snow until he was convinced of the problem. "Yep, there's depth hoar, but not much here," he agreed. "I think it's worth taking a chance on at least to Cache Ledge."

I was less than enthusiastic about the risk. I told him to go ahead, but I would not move farther until the snow had settled or broken loose.

Loaded with camp and personal gear, Willi and Peter slowly crept up the fixed line and out of sight. They had to pull each rope free from under the heavy snowfall of the previous night.

Andy and Devi appeared from below, climbing slowly toward us. They made a good pair. They would be three or four hours behind several of us who preferred to get the carry over with before the sun became intolerable. They spent rest days, as well as carrying days, in each other's company. They were becoming inseparable.

Climbers often gravitate to those who react the same to danger, carrying, and leading. We could all see that Devi and Andy shared more than an interest in climbing. There was a mutual trust between the two. They had the same relaxed personalities and seemed determined to enjoy the mountain with each other. Devi and Andy were falling in love.

Relationships on a mountain can be a hindrance. As Devi and Andy grew closer, neither would carry a load without the other. On rest days or sick days the expedition lost two climbers rather than one. It was a source of annoyance to those of us giving the climb everything we had.

That morning had been an unusual one for Devi. The porters had asked her to participate in a Hindu ceremony called *Rakhi*.

The religious rite is performed to ensure that the men of the family will defend a woman's life and honor as a member of the household. The woman—or in some cases a holy man—ties a string around the wrist of the man. This wristlet protects him from harm. *Rakhi* is usually performed each year by the sister in each family. Since the porters were away from home, Devi would substitute nicely.

The porters had paid Devi one rupee each to have her tie a string around their wrists. Kiran, Nirmal, Lou, and Andy had also taken part. She insisted Jim and I have one tied on our wrists, but because we didn't have a rupee she promised to find one at Advanced Base and pretend it was ours.

We were all in a playful mood. Andy and I took pictures of Jim practicing medicine, including one posed photograph of Jim using one of our three-foot tubular pickets on me for a rectal exam. Few times in the past month had we laughed so hard.

Jim had needed a rest day and a change of partners. He would be ready to go hard in the morning, so we planned a 2:00 A.M. start to catch Willi and Peter and carry ropes for them. An early dinner and a sleeping pill ended a long, but restful, day.

"It's really blowing out there, but it's clear," I said, searching for my clothes. "Seems colder than usual too."

"What time is it?" Jim mumbled.

"One-thirty. I'll start cooking."

The wind tore at the tent. Spindrift sounded like sandpaper against the frozen nylon. The candle wouldn't stay lit in the tent, so Jim held his headlamp onto the cooking area. The light danced through the dense fog of our cold breath.

I heated ice and listened to the sputtering of the Phoebus stove, which gave at least the illusion of warmth. We huddled in our down bags, patiently waiting for the water to boil. Soon we were dressed. Outside the tent, our frozen fingers clawed at crampons, ice axes, and packs. Thoughts of getting back into my sleeping bag never left my mind. We shouldered heavy loads of rope and started up.

My ears crackled with infection, and when I breathed my throat was raw. I fastened my jumars to the first rope and checked them twice to be sure in the blackness. My mind was drifting. I began to pull on the rope and crawl through the deep wind-pack of snow.

The snow became hard and easy to ascend several rope lengths later. We made up for lost time and arrived at Cache Ledge fifty minutes after leaving Camp I. Willi and Peter were only three hundred feet away, traversing under the large rock wall. We heard but seldom saw them in the starlight. I raced along and caught Willi at the beginning of Jim's Lead. An hour later, Willi, Peter, Jim, and I stood at the end of the fixed lines.

"We had a real bad night," said Willi as we waited in the dark for Peter to finish the first lead. "The wind darn near tore us off the mountain."

Placing ice screws and pins for protection, Peter climbed a steep narrow ice hose. He became only a shadow on the rope and an occasional clink of metal, like a ghost with chains. Soon even the sounds were gone as he traversed several hundred feet away.

Jim had waited below until Peter finished the pitch, then he joined me. Willi left to follow Peter.

"My feet are freezing waiting around." Jim's teeth chattered. "I wouldn't mind moving a little faster."

Willi yelled for me to remove the pins so he could continue over to Peter and take the next lead. I started jumaring to stay warm and soon reached Peter belaying at a small stance. It was sheltered by a small rock roof.

"Nice lead, Peter," I said. "The best on the route so far."

Jim came up and we huddled together for the extra warmth. Peter had placed three bombproof pins, so I tied off to these, then dug under the roof for what turned out to be a great place to put our loads of rope.

Jim had chopped and dug himself a good stance, but his feet were still freezing. "Let's cache the ropes here and start down, John. Willi's going to be pretty slow on this pitch."

I had to agree. Willi was having difficulty with the deep sugar snow and was still only fifty feet out.

"O.K., there's no reason for the four of us to be here. Peter, there's enough rope here for twelve hundred more feet of climbing. I hope you use it," I kidded.

By now it was daylight. Jim and I moved quickly down the ropes to the top of Jim's Lead. There, I had my first view of Peter's "escape route." Peter had just shown us how good a climber he really was by his last lead over ice-encrusted rock, yet here was a mistake we could ill afford. Not only was the traverse exposed to rockfall and avalanche, but it also wasted six hundred feet of rope and many rock pins, of which we were desperately short.

"Peter can take that mess down tomorrow, while we're leading," I said to Jim. "I'm not going to carry rope and hardware up here to be wasted like that."

"Don't count on it. Peter's not about to remove that mess. He still believes it will be useful later on."

Jim was right. The "escape route" remained intact.

Jim descended quickly back to temporary Camp II (Cache Ledge) while I cleaned the extra pins and webbing from the fixed points. We needed the hardware for the Buttress—nothing could be wasted.

After a quick lunch at Camp II, we rappeled to Camp I in time for the 2:00 P.M. radio call. Devi, Andy, and Nirmal had just arrived from below.

"Good news!" Lou vibrated with excitement over the radio. "Roskelley, your messiah is at Base Camp. Evans arrived and he brought the mail and extra rope!"

"Fantastic!" we yelled. The news was almost too good to be true. "Did Jim get a letter from his dad? He wants to know, and while you're at it, count how many letters I got. Yahoo!"

Evans had arrived at Base the previous day. He sent two porters up with rope and the mail that morning, so only Lou, Kiran, and our high-altitude porters had learned of the news. The others descended immediately upon hearing mail was at Advanced Base.

"By the way," Lou continued, "I sent the two porters and their dog out to catch Ad. From what Evans says, Ad is still waiting at Romani for them. How's the route coming?"

"Willi and Peter had a long way to go when we left them," I explained. "They won't reach the North Ridge today. Say, we don't need Peter's second route up there . . . why don't you say something?"

"O.K., I'll talk with him tonight."

All that we had prayed for, discussed at meals, and worried about at night had suddenly appeared in one moment. The emotional charge was overpowering. Everything we needed had come.

Willi called in at 7:00 P.M. from Camp II with exciting news on the route. "Peter put up the hardest pitch yet, over ice-covered rock. We think we got to within two pitches of the North Ridge. We're beat though, and neither of us can continue tomorrow."

"Great job you guys!" Lou said. "John and Jim can have a go at the Ridge tomorrow then."

Lou told them about Evans, the mail, and the rope.

"That's the best news we've heard in weeks!" Willi exclaimed.

"Peter, did you clean up your escape route?" Lou asked. "We'll need that rope and hardware up higher."

"That's a useable route!" Peter insisted. "I put it there in case of avalanche conditions."

"We feel it's unnecessary Peter. The other route is just as safe," Lou argued.

Willi came back on the radio. "We'll take care of it later. Right now the important thing is to get to the North Ridge."

Evans came in on the radio from Base and said hello to everyone. He said his wife had given birth to a boy before he departed.

The weather again looked promising at dusk. After a dinner of freeze-dried beef, corn, and potatoes, Jim and I struggled to get some sleep.

Sleeping is a problem for most high-altitude climbers due to a phenomenon known as "Cheyne-Stokes breathing." While dozing, the climber breathes normally for a minute, then stops completely for thirty seconds. Suddenly, breathing resumes at an accelerated rate. One minute you sound out of breath, the next, dead. It is often more disconcerting for the tentmate than the sleeper.

Sleeping hours also change. To avoid daylight heat or the common afternoon Himalayan storms, teams will climb at night. Midnight or 1:00 A.M. wake-ups are common.

Everyone had their own way of getting to sleep. For Jim, it was sleeping pills. For most, it was exhaustion. I'm a light sleeper, so even pills didn't work for me. I could go on several hours of sleep a day for a week, then finally enjoy a good night's rest. I preferred moving up the route to lying in the sack.

"Jim." I poked his sleeping bag about the shoulders. "It's one o'clock. Better get ready."

It was another clear morning. While I began dressing, Jim leaned forward, pumped the stove, and lit the starter gas.

"How's your throat?" Jim asked.

"Pretty sore. My ears are draining and crackling all the time, too."

"Better start the penicillin."

Jim flicked his wrist and the stove roared to life. As it melted the snow we had collected the night before, we dressed awkwardly. It was impossible to stay in our sleeping bags and dress completely.

We consumed a hot meal of oatmeal and cocoa before pulling on our boots and gaiters and leaving the security of the tent. By memory we found our crampons and gear, slipped into our harnesses, and loaded our packs for the day.

"Why don't you start, Jim," I suggested. "I want to take it as easy as possible on my throat."

Jim found the start of the fixed line and began the daily routine of punching through the wind-packed crust. We jumared close together by starlight. I could hear his crampons bite, crunching on hard snow and ice when he didn't punch through. A rasping, harsh breathing sliced the eerie silence as he worked.

Ice formed around my beard, moustache, and eyelids. A sharp wind whipped spindrift into my eyes and through the openings of my clothing.

We stopped often to rest or to change our jumar from one rope to another. The stop was always short because our sweat would freeze immediately. Neither of us spoke; each moved silently in his own world, aware only of the next step or change of rope. We arrived at the precariously positioned tent of Camp II.

"Peter?" I whispered.

"Yeah?"

"Are you guys going down today?" I asked.

"Yes," he said. "We're burned out."

Willi wished us luck as I continued up the ropes. The snow conditions were superb out on the large open slope below Jim's Lead. We were moving well. I was pumping air like a long-distance runner.

Lightning flashed in the west and my mind began to wander. *Jim's setting a good pace . . . my throat's killing me . . . I wonder if I'll be healthy enough to continue? . . . We've got to make the North Ridge today . . . Is everyone back home O.K.? . . . Where is my wife?* I tried to recall what day of the week it was. I couldn't. Jim and I were both feasting on thoughts that would take us far away from exhaustion, cold, and danger.

We reached the end of the fixed lines at daybreak. The shadow of Nanda Devi, which had stretched for hundreds of miles to the west an hour ago, was shrinking back into the Sanctuary. Soon the sun's height would erase the shadow completely.

Peter's last lead had been difficult. Even following it on jumars was a chore. As I set up the belay, Jim arrived at the small stance.

"When I get to the end of my lead and tie you off, I'll

give the rope two hard jerks," I whispered. I didn't have a voice. My throat was too sore and constricted.

Jim untangled the belay line, tied himself to the end, and watched as I carefully swam upward through deep sugar snow over steep rock. I fought my way out of one blind gully to another, climbing rock, icc, or both to avoid the snow. Toward the head of a major gully I angled steeply left to a large, open, forty-degree slope. The technical difficulties ended, but wading upward through deep snow at 21,000 feet was draining my energy fast.

The snow felt ready to slide, so I aimed for a small rock outcrop, hoping to find a crack for a belay point. Three hundred feet out and at the end of the rope, I reached the rock, found a perfect crack, and anchored the line. Jim ascended slowly, exhausted from the effort of jumaring in the bottomless snow.

"I'm beat," he gasped. "Unless you want to try, I'm for going back down."

I fished into my pack for another rope, uncoiled it, and handed the rope to Jim. "Here, I'll take it for another three hundred feet." I was determined to get to the North Ridge.

The sun was on us as I floundered through thigh-deep snow around our belay rock to a low-angled rib crest. Two hundred feet out, I reached the next grouping of quartzite blocks. The avalanche danger diminished. I continued climbing short slabs and steep, narrow gullies, and finally reached another precarious belay.

Jim climbed toward me at a snail's pace, but when he arrived, he announced he would lead the next pitch.

Now the sun was punishing us. I hid my head behind a small corner for relief as Jim took the rack of hardware. Inside three short vertical walls, he fought his way up through the first fifteen feet of bottomless spindrift snow. He chimneyed up and over with difficulty until he stood on the slope above. He rested, then slowly waded to a rock outcrop the shape of an eyebrow, and buried a pin deep into a crack. He clipped in and rested again.

Jim traversed up with a swimming motion through the snow, but was stopped short. The belay line was caught somewhere below me. I pulled and flipped the rope until it came free, then Jim continued floundering upward and out of sight.

The jerking on the belay line had awakened me. In my exhausted daze I had slipped into unconsciousness. The combination of heat, my ear infection, and exhaustion put me in a euphoric daze. I slapped some ice into my mouth and patted my cheeks with snow to stay awake.

The rope had stopped one hundred feet out. Jim must have run into some problem, I thought. With a subtle finality, the rope began to snake back down to me as slowly as it had payed out. Jim came into view, backed down over the outcrop, and stopped at his piton.

"Lower me off the pin," he mumbled, too exhausted to speak plainly.

I lowered him carefully to where I stood.

"The slope above is dangerous," he said. "I'm too tired to fight it."

"O.K., let's get back to camp."

We had struggled hard. We had been climbing steadily for twelve hours but the deep snow, heat, and exhaustion had stopped us short of the Ridge. I set my rappel system and descended, staggering and falling. When the rope went slack, Jim followed. Communication between us was impossible because of my lost voice, but we didn't need it anyway. We were in our own worlds.

A vicious wind picked up at the bottom of our second rappel. Clouds blotted out the sun and by the time I started to reverse Peter's last lead, a steady avalanche of new snow was cascading down the gully we were in. It began to snow hard. Rappel after rappel, we tried desperately to stay on our feet and keep out of the avalanches to our right. As if the heat hadn't been bad enough, we were now freezing in our own sweat. We stopped at the cache where we had left Peter the day before. It sheltered us from the avalanches breaking loose all around us.

"What do you think we should do?" I asked.

"I'm worried that open slope below will break loose on us. We ought to get started down before there's a big buildup of snow and we have to bivouac here."

A bivouac didn't sound inviting. "Let's get down," I

agreed. I unclipped and traversed onto the first open slope.

The storm continued to dump snow at an alarming rate as we made it to Jim's Lead. Four rappels took us to the safety of the cliff where Camp II was perched. Nothing big had broken loose, although we had withstood several large sloughs. Luck had been with us.

The camp was empty. Willi and Peter had descended to Advanced Base to rest. The quietness of the sheltered camp was strange compared to what we had just been through on the slopes. We were beat. An hour later, we made the short descent to Camp I.

Lou smiled as he munched on a candy bar and greeted us at the end of the ropes. "Good to see you guys. Pretty rough weather this afternoon. How'd it go?"

I flopped down next to our tent. "It's a burnout from here. We got to within three hundred feet of the Ridge, but the slope was too dangerous and we were too tired to get there."

"We're going to have to move to a higher camp in order to make the North Ridge without exhausting ourselves," Jim continued. "I could see the Ridge and it's easy from our high point."

Lou was visibly disappointed. He was sure we had made the Ridge that day because Pete and Willi had said they were only several hundred feet from it the day before.

"Well," he said, "Devi and I will lead tomorrow and Kiran and Nirmal will carry. They're all here at Camp I."

Indeed, four tents were now pitched in camp.

"I'm going to take a breather tomorrow, Lou," I said. "I'm pretty tired."

I hid my real reason. My ear infection was beginning to hurt and my sore throat made it impossible to speak, but I still wanted to carry.

Jim decided to go down to rest for several days. He had worked hard with Peter and Willi for days and then with me. Now was the best time for a break.

"Say, here's your mail," Lou said, smiling. He handed it over to us. "I knew this would cheer you up."

Jim and I clutched the bundles of letters and went to our tent. Tears streamed down our faces as we uncovered each bit of news from home.

It was one of the happiest days of the expedition. With the arrival of Evans, the rope, and the mail, the entire expedition had taken a turn for the better. We were finally making progress.

NINE

Throughout the night of the fourteenth, blasts of wind and heavy snows buffeted Camp I. Spindrift buried the three tents so that one of us was out shoveling every hour. The buildup of snow pushed in the tent walls and ceilings until the interiors were half their normal size. Lou, Devi, Jim, Nirmal, Kiran, and I huddled inside our tents. Lou called out from his tent that he didn't think anyone would be moving in the morning, including himself. But, unable to suffocate in his tent any longer, he eventually came over to our tent at dawn to eat breakfast and shovel us free.

"Good morning," Kiran said on his way to the toilet. "Bloody bad day, eh?"

"Sure is, Kiran," I said. "Jim and I will pass breakfast through the back door to you and Nirmal. Be careful you don't slide down to Advanced Base while relieving yourself!"

As we cooked breakfast, Jim was in a turmoil. His mood and desire for solitude were evident—he needed to be alone. Himalayan climbers have to learn to exist in a four-by-seven-by-four-foot space: noise, smells, flapping tent walls, bumping each other, cold, and darkness all contribute to personality changes. If the problem isn't solved, the climb can end early or feuds develop. Despite the hours a climber endures alone at the end of a rope, he or she craves a peaceful, relaxing solitude once in camp. Jim wanted to descend to Advanced Base, but even there he would have to face Willi's and Pete's sarcasms.

Later, during morning radio call from Advanced Base, Willi asked Jim to come down and look at a porter who was coughing up bloody sputum. Over the radio, Jim diagnosed the problem as a possible pulmonary embolism, a clot from the leg that had moved into the lungs. He told Willi what to do for the porter, but remained unsure if he would descend to have a look right then.

It had stopped snowing, but the weather still looked threatening. I didn't think the snow conditions were stable enough for Jim to descend and advised him against it. Uncharacteristically, I wanted the company. We ended up talking and reading the rest of the day, and I pumped penicillin tablets every hour to kill my ear infection.

Meanwhile, Devi's cough continued and worsened. She considered going down to Advanced Base with Jim. Nirmal and Kiran, however, were determined to stick it out at Camp I with Lou and me.

The day dragged by. We read, napped, made small talk. Later in the afternoon wet snow began to fall. It continued into the night long after I had fallen asleep. Periodically, I was awakened by a feeling of claustrophobia as the heavy snow crushed the ceiling of the tent. Jim and I took turns hitting the ceiling and pushing against the walls to keep them from collapsing. It was still dark inside the tent when we awoke in the morning.

With twelve inches of new snow, it looked like another rest day. Lou cleared several of the ropes above camp while we fed the others porridge. The next order of business was to find our tools. The snow shovel was nowhere in sight and Lou searched frantically for it. He found it buried under the fresh snow. While clearing the camp, Jim realized his ice axe was missing. The five of us dug for an hour to discover my axe but not Jim's.

That afternoon, Jim finally left for Advanced Base despite a hail storm. I sensed he wanted to be alone for a few days before returning to lead or carry loads. He deserved the overdue rest.

With Jim's departure, I had gained some solitude. I retired to my tent to write letters. It was now like a home: I could relax, rest, and kill my infection.

On his way down the ropes, Jim encountered Andy carrying a load to Camp I. Conditions were terrible. Deep wet snow hampered movement in either direction and

Andy wisely decided to abandon his attempt to reach Camp I. He returned to Advanced Base with Jim.

After dinner, those of us left at Camp I retired to the darkness of our tents. I found a little warmth flickering in a candle I had brought with me. Little things seemed so amazing in the world in which we were now living—one small candle could light an entire two-man tent. I began to look to its flame for companionship. It was warm, friendly, and its flickering was a sign of life in an otherwise cold and harsh world. It didn't take up any room, was quiet, and had a pleasant odor. I could even put it to sleep and it wouldn't roll over and wake me.

The third day of the storm brought little relief to anyone except me. The storm was the break I had needed to recuperate; my ear and sore throat improved considerably with the warm air of the tent and heavy doses of drugs. For the others it was a time of boredom and low morale. Days of staying in camp became disheartening. With such a long way to go to the summit, most of the team needed to work, not sit.

Lou and Devi descended to Advanced Base early that morning. Devi's sore throat had not improved and she decided it would get better only at a lower altitude. Needing some exercise, Lou went along to pick up a load, meet John Evans, and return that same evening. Kiran and Nirmal disappeared up the ropes to pull them free from the heavy snows of the past few days. I sacked out after cooking breakfast.

In midafternoon, Lou plodded into camp exhausted from his three-and-a-half hour effort to climb back to Camp I.

"Come on in, Lou," I suggested. "I'll cook some fish and noodles for us."

"Great! I haven't eaten all day. The porters down at Advanced Base ran out of wood to cook with, so I didn't eat breakfast. They even burned some boxes before they got the energy to go down to Base and get more wood. But they needed to make the trip anyway to get Evans's gear and the extra porter food."

"I can't believe they crossed that glacier after all the snow we've had."

"Yeah, but they made it safely."

That evening, Devi related a strange problem to us over the radio. She could hardly control her laughter. "The porters have decided that the weather is bad because we are eating beef on the mountain."

"Hey, Kiran!" I shouted. "Did you hear that?"

"What the bloody hell?!" he exploded. "I am eating beef and I am the highest caste of Brahmin! What insolence! If *I* can eat it, they can! On a mountain in adversity, you can eat anything—even human flesh!"

The porters were down at Base with Willi and Evans so we would have to wait for their reply to his outburst. We were sure Kiran would convince them with his human flesh argument. Beef or no beef, there was no end in sight to the bad weather. Snow again put us to sleep.

The sky was overcast the following morning. Although it was warmer, a thick cloud layer enveloped the upper and lower slopes of the mountain. Snow had stopped falling.

Snuggled deep in my bag, I could hear Lou shoveling around the tents. Soon he had worked his way to mine and after much rustling about with the tent-door zipper his bearded face and floppy white stocking cap suddenly appeared. We decided to carry to Cache Ledge and clear the ropes.

The ropes had an inch of wind-packed crust over them, yet it took us only one-and-a-half hours to reach the lonely tent at Cache Ledge.

"Good thing we came up Lou," I said. "This tent is damn near buried."

Spindrift and avalanche debris had pushed one tent wall clear to the floor. The thin fiberglass wands had flexed but had not broken. To our amazement, the aluminum poles we had had manufactured were still erect and in fine condition.

We worked for several hours clearing snow from around the tent. It was pitched so precariously on such a tiny ledge that it was all we could do to hang on and clear the side closest to the rock wall. We dug out the entrance as deep as possible so we could enter easily.

A quick descent brought us back to camp in time for the two o'clock radio call.

"How are things down below?" Lou asked.

"O.K.," Jim replied. "Willi, Evans, and the porters are finally arriving on the other side of the glacier. Looks like they're going to cross . . . Yep, here they come."

At that moment, Lou and I heard the grating and rumbling of an avalanche on its way to the Rishi—perfect timing to catch the group crossing the glacier.

"Jim!" Lou cried over the radio, "an avalanche is just passing us. Tell Willi to turn back!"

We jumped out of our tent to watch the scene unfold several thousand feet below. We could see and hear someone at Advanced Base yelling at the others on the glacier. The little band of men understood and began scrambling off the ice just as the avalanche leaped off the snout and roared by them.

They couldn't have been crossing at a worse time of day. An earlier start from Base would have been wiser. They waited for some minutes, then started across again. Jim told us they were safely across at 2:30 P.M. During the twenty minutes it took the group to climb to Advanced Base, seven more slides came down. The avalanches continued for the next two hours.

"Willi," Jim asked later, "how did you know there wasn't going to be a slide when you came across?"

"The old master knows," he smiled and answered.

"Take your own chances, Willi," Jim advised, "but don't take a chance with the porters' lives. They trust our judgment to make the right decisions."

Back at Camp I, Kiran and Nirmal insisted on cooking the evening meal for us. They collected the stoves and pots to cook a meat and noodle dinner. Although Lou and I argued with them, it did no good. I thought we would be minus one tent by the time they were through, but nothing caught fire. We told them they were cooking too much but they had to see for themselves. Lou and I choked down double servings because we knew the Indians would be offended if all the food weren't eaten.

Nirmal was not as happy as before, but we suspected this was due to his rank in the Indian army. Even under expedition circumstances, Nirmal was still a sergeant and of lower caste than Kiran. We liked our Indian companions. They were relaxed and very quiet around us, trying hard to please. But their climbing safety methods and slowness remained troublesome.

Another day disappeared and snow fell again during the night.

Both sides of my tent were pushed in to their limits that morning. To avoid being smothered in my sleep, I had involuntarily moved to the center of the tent. Small spindrift avalanches hit the camp in addition to the continual barrage of heavier avalanches sweeping the open face.

"Hey, John," Lou yelled, his voice muffled by the snow on both our tents. "I don't think we're moving again this morning."

"No shit," I yelled back. "We're damn near buried alive right here."

I dressed and crawled out into a swirling mass of blowing snow. A spindrift avalanche dropped on me and snow spilled into the cracks in my jacket and booties. I could barely see Lou's tent ten yards away. I plunged to my waist through snow along the cliff to the latrine. Using my axe for safety, I managed to reverse my path even wearing the slick leather-bottomed down booties. For the next hour I dug out my tent and part of the Indians', who were still lingering in the sack. My finale was a narrow trail to Lou's door.

"Say," Lou said, looking up from his book, "if American trains were as dependable as those avalanches, we would lead the world."

"They never stop, do they? Why don't you come over for breakfast? You can help me wrestle the stoves away from Kiran."

A roar came from across the mountain face as I spoke. A serac had broken loose and had started a monster slide.

"There's one for Advanced Base," I remarked. "That'll wake 'em up."

At Advanced Base, Jim, Willi, and Evans were just rising in the four-man tent. Peter, alone in a two-man, and Devi and Andy, also in a two-man tent, were still sleeping. The noise of the avalanche scared them. They weren't prepared for the ferocious wind blast that followed.

The blast almost collapsed the four-man tent, bending many of the poles again. Willi and Jim bent back the poles while Evans dug out the tents and a new platform area. Within an hour the camp was back to normal.

"Advanced Base, do you read?" I called.

"Advanced Base here, Rascal," Willi replied.

"Rascal" was a nickname Peter had tagged me with early in the trip. Several of the others, particularly Willi, were soon using it to distinguish me from John Evans.

"How did you like the freight train we sent you this morning?" I joked.

"That was a real blast, John," Willi laughed. "We appreciate everything you guys do for us."

I ended the conversation and turned my attention to cooking the morning's oatmeal. Hour after hour passed slowly. Evans had been thoughtful enough to bring in several *Time* magazines, which we all read cover to cover, two or three times. We read everything we could find, right down to the instructions on our film canisters.

Snow continued to fall and we fell asleep to the rumbling of avalanches down the mountain face.

August 19 was even worse than the previous days. It snowed more. Our camp and our spirits were buried. The tents resembled snow tunnels with doors; it took Lou and me four diggings a day to keep even with the snowfall.

During the middle of the night Lou shifted the head of his bag to the entrance of his tent so he wouldn't suffocate if the tent collapsed under the snow's weight. He slept easier. I enjoyed listening to the rumble of slides that cut loose through the night. Their wind blasts now did little harm to our well-protected camp.

"Hey Kiran," Lou chimed in between the roar of snowslides, "we may have to have a human sacrifice to pacify the gods if they're offended by beef eaters on the mountain. You may have to play the starring role!"

Kiran took the joking in stride and gave us back a little

of our own medicine. Nirmal didn't understand, however, until Kiran translated, and laughter burst from the Indians' tent.

Soon after a two-hour dig-out in the afternoon, a sudden appearance of sunshine gave us new hope. Lou, Kiran, and I dragged out our cameras to take pictures of the spectacular peaks with their fresh coverings of snow. The sun, with its warmth and light, sparked our desire to climb again. Talk of quitting the mountain ended as suddenly as it had started. After all, the storm couldn't last forever.

Lou quickly sketched the new logistics for the climb above Camp I. He and I would move to Cache Ledge, now considered Camp II, while several of the others at Advanced Base would take our places at Camp I. At last, the weather appeared to be improving.

August 20 was clear, bright, and windless. The camp buzzed with activity as Lou, Nirmal, Kiran, and I readied for the carry. Lou and I were carrying our personal gear in order to stay at the upper camp, while the two Indians would carry group gear in support.

The ropes were buried deep and we moved slowly. I broke the first 150-foot stretch, sinking to my thighs. The fresh loose powder had to be cleared by hand, then crushed down with the knees. Only then could I swim forward using the rope, which was buried several feet, to progress twelve inches.

Lou led the next pitch, which took close to an hour. This ended at an avalanche gully that was packed from heavy powder slides. The gully ended on the steeper slopes of the face, but this was still easier going than the first leads of the morning.

We arrived exhausted at Camp II. The tent was still intact, albeit slightly crushed from the snow. We spent several hours making our new home livable, complete with a good stance for the latrine and a lowered front porch for easier entering. Willi and Peter had kept the tent perfectly clean during their previous stay.

Kiran and Nirmal appeared hours after we had reached the camp. Due to the terrible conditions, they were exceedingly slow. We welcomed them in for tea and snacks we found stashed at the new camp.

Although Cache Ledge was originally a temporary camp, it was now considered a necessary stop before the North Ridge. This bit of news was music to Pete's ears, since Lou and I had condemned the idea at first but were now glad the camp was there.

Everyone was moving on the mountain. Devi and Andy moved to Camp I, while Peter, Willi, and John Evans carried in support with intentions of descending back to Advanced Base Camp. Jim's diarrhea was still a problem, so he helped the porters retrieve loads of wood from Ridge Camp.

We made considerable progress on the mountain in one day. Lou and I had occupied a higher camp and many loads had been carried. The day ended with a beautiful sunset. Intending to make a bid for the Ridge the next day, Lou and I ate an early dinner and went to sleep. My ear and throat had cleared during the six-day storm; I felt strong and sure we would reach the Ridge the next morning.

The night had been peaceful and we expected a beautiful day. At 2:00 A.M. Lou switched on his headlamp and started breakfast.

An hour and a half later we crawled from the tent to start ascending the ropes. I stepped over to the fixed line and started the awkward traverse to the open slopes. The going was worse than ever. A hard inch-thick crust had to be broken to pull the rope free, making for laborious, time-consuming work.

The air was crisp and clear around the Garhwal. Lightning was firing in the west over Nanda Kot. It seemed as though a war was raging and we were the only spectators.

We had underestimated the difficulty of uncovering the buried ropes and this prevented us from gaining ground quickly. Our gear was murderously heavy. Lou broke lead after lead, while I followed with the heavier load. It took us an hour for every three-hundred-foot rope length.

At the end of my first lead since the week past, the sun

beat us into exhausted submission. We could not push ourselves any farther that day. Dumping the rope and hardware, we retreated back to Camp II. We would have to try for the Ridge again the next day.

Kiran and Nirmal had continued to the top of Jim's Lead and dropped their loads, attached to several anchors. They also had succumbed to the heat. Jim and Peter moved to Camp I, leaving Willi and Evans at Advanced Base to come the next day. Everyone had accomplished something.

Meanwhile, a goat had been killed at Base and the porters brought the meat up to Camp I. Lou and I got what was left after those at Advanced Base and Camp I had their fill. Devi and Andy brought some scraps to our tent door at Camp II, then spent most of the day there resting.

It had become obvious to most of the team that Devi and Andy were more than just teammates. They were constant companions, whether in camp or on the ropes. Since any teammate's action affects all the other climbers, Andy's and Devi's relationship became a concern of ours. As their relationship grew, so did the talk about it. I thought it was a potentially damaging relationship; now was no time to fragment the group further.

It was 2:15 A.M. when Lou and I awoke. Fighting the darkness and fatigue, we started quickly up yesterday's broken tracks. In three hours we reached our high point of the day before.

Two and a half hours later, after sharing the leading of the last 450 feet of easy snow slope, we reached the crest of the North Ridge at 9:00 A.M. Unnamed, unclimbed peaks unfolded before us. Tibet, its brownish red wastelands stretching to the northeast, shimmered in the early morning sun. Familiar peaks—Changabang, Kalenka, Kamet, even Dhaulagiri—rose in the distance.

Lou and I felt good and relaxed on the broad flat crest that ran at a low angle to the Buttress a half mile away. The Ridge would make a superb Camp III. Just getting this far was a true accomplishment.

TEN

Clearly visible from our position on the Ridge, the Buttress was obviously a serious problem. Lou thought it similar to the South Face of the Washington Column in Yosemite Valley, but at an altitude of 23,000 to 24,000 feet. I searched out a possible route up the center. The more I studied the problem, the better the center looked.

"What do you think, John?" Lou asked skeptically.

"It looks like there's a route on the rib of the Buttress leading to the gully halfway. I think it'll go, but I'll need Jim. We've climbed together on ground like this before. I think we can move pretty fast."

Lou and I spent several hours acclimatizing and enjoying the view before we returned to Camp II down the long series of ropes that we knew by heart. On our descent we found Jim at the top of Jim's Lead. He had just completed a carry and had stopped there. To our dismay, Peter, Andy, Devi, Kiran, Nirmal, and now even Jim, had dumped their loads too low; they should have been carried two pitches farther to the small overhang we called "Roskelley Dump." Without thinking, I yelled at Jim for dropping his load so low. Though not pointed at Jim specifically, the incident caused more ill feelings.

Jim and Kiran had moved up to Camp II while Lou and I were surveying the Buttress. For two hours, we helped them excavate another tent site, a difficult task considering the short width of the snow cone on which we perched.

Lou and I were poised to move to the Ridge in the morning. Knowing we had strong support in Kiran and

Jim, we sacked out early. The clear starry night promised good weather.

The four of us at Camp II were up and ready by 4:00 A.M. August 23 was blustery and overcast. We attached crampons and started across the traverse, but a steady snowfall convinced us to return to camp and take a rest day.

"Hello!" Willi yelled from the ropes. "Anyone there?"

"Come on over," Lou answered.

Willi, John Evans, and two porters had carried up from Camp I. After a short discussion about weather, they continued up to Roskelley Dump, unloaded, and returned. At Camp II, Jim, Kiran, Lou, and I went back to sleep feeling guilty for not continuing. In the afternoon I ascended the ropes to the start of Jim's Lead and returned, cleaning the route of loose rope and extra pitons.

Now that we needed rope and pins, the problem of what to do about Peter's escape route returned. Peter had been working on it again when we had been descending from the Ridge; he was determined that his route would stay. Andy had tried Pete's route, however, and found it dangerous and uncomfortable. Peter exploded at Lou and me at Camp II on his way to his own camp. We apologized for yelling about the loads being dumped at the wrong site, but insisted his route had wasted too much equipment and was not safe. Again we could not agree and the issue remained unresolved. The route was left in place, never to be used.

The bad weather, cold, crowded tents, wet clothing, and constant danger gave us all a persistent empty, nervous feeling. The conditions contributed to our frequent outbursts. Kiran summed it up when he said our emotions were extremes—either extremely conscientious or extremely impolite. Anyone could be a target.

With his clear, pleasant voice, lively eyes, and wagging moustache, Kiran entertained us that night with his stories. Even when the night got too cold to sit without a sleeping bag, he kept us listening. He told us about his life in the army for the last ten years. It had been hard on his family, who could not be with him at his post in Kashmir. His greatest disappointment, however, was missing the conflict with the Pakistanis while he was on an expedition to Bhutan. He related story after story of his experiences with the commando paratroops in Northern India.

Despite his willingness to eat beef, Kiran was deeply religious. He believed that God would protect him from danger in the mountains as he followed in the footsteps of his older brother "Bull" Kumar, one of India's best climbers and leader of many Himalayan ascents. He was a yoga disciple and was trained in all the Hindu virtues of routine and self-control. Kiran's belief in God's protection was tested frequently, as he had suffered serious injury in the mountains several times. On the 1974 Changabang expedition, Kiran fell three hundred feet and almost died. His injuries kept him from the summit.

We turned in to get an early start again to the Ridge. Lou and I would plan to stay and Jim and Kiran would carry camp gear in support.

The wind was beginning to rip across the North Ridge as Jim, Lou, and I arrived exhausted but happy on the crest. It was 9:00 A.M., five hours after we had started from Camp II. We eagerly excavated a tent platform on the broad back of the Ridge. We found a sheltered cove away from the small cornices overhanging the North Slope and pitched the two-man tent.

"I'm going to take a close look at the Buttress," Lou said. "I'll be back soon." He plowed methodically through deep snow along the wide spine of the Ridge until he became only a moving dot, a speck against the awesome Buttress.

We had not seen Kiran since early morning. He was carrying a load from Camp II, but had started later than we had.

"Say, John," Jim said, turning to me as he readied to descend, "what'll I tell Kiran if I see him still coming?"

The wind had picked up and I didn't like the looks of the sky to the south. "Tell him to cache his load at Roskelley Dump and descend. Lou and I will pick it up tomorrow. But I can't imagine he would still be coming this late."

Jim disappeared down the fixed lines in a swirling mass of powder snow, moving slowly and cautiously because of fatigue. Lou and I ducked into our tent and began to melt snow for dinner.

"Hello! Hello!" Kiran's voice swept by in the wind.

"Over here!" we yelled.

Several minutes elapsed before Kiran stumbled into the shallow depression that protected our tent. It was 2:00 P.M. Kiran dropped his pack, then unloaded the supplies he had struggled so desperately with since early morning.

"Come on in, Kiran," we invited. "Here, have some tea. Maybe you should spend the night here?"

"No, I'll be fine," he gasped. "I'm just not used to the altitude and got a late start."

"Didn't Jim tell you to cache your load?" I asked.

"Yes, but I wanted to see how far I could go."

Lou was stunned and slightly annoyed that Kiran had pushed on and taken a chance to reach the Ridge. My doubts about Kiran's judgment were compounding. He didn't seem to know when the mountain had the advantage. His spiritual and physical strength far overpowered his common sense; until he learned that his safety came first, he would endanger himself and the entire team. Lou asked him not to try something like that again. Kiran agreed amiably and readied himself to leave. At 3:00 P.M., Kiran descended in a howling blizzard.

Meanwhile, Jim rappeled to the top of Jim's Lead just as Peter arrived from below. He was thoroughly irritated when he saw Peter had taken the lighter, already used and open, food bag from Camp II. Jim and Kiran needed that food for several more days. Little was said as Jim grabbed some freeze-dried food, jerky, and jello from the bag and continued on his way down. Devi, Willi, John Evans, Andy, and Jatendra were still carrying as Jim descended. Half an hour later, he was back in camp.

"Camp Two, this is Three," Lou radioed at 5:00 P.M. "Kiran insisted on leaving here at three o'clock. Has he arrived at Camp Two yet?"

"No, haven't seen him," Jim answered. "Willi and

Devi are still above, so he may be with them. Peter will go out to the corner and take a look."

"You should have stayed with him, Jim," Peter reprimanded. "You just don't leave someone up there alone."

"Bullshit. I told him to cache his load and descend, but he insisted on going higher. I can't order him down."

The situation was becoming serious. Chances were good that Kiran may have made an error and was either stuck along the ropes between Camp II and III or, exhausted, had sat down and frozen to death in the cold wind. It was beginning to look like a case of déjà vu.

A friend of Kiran's, Harsh Bahuguna, had frozen to death on Mount Everest's Southwest Face during a fierce storm in 1971. Exhausted, Harsh had succumbed to the intense cold and wind while traversing a fixed rope to a lower camp. A rescue party reached him several hours after his disappearance, but was unable to lower the unconscious man. They were forced to leave him to die as the storm intensified and threatened their own lives.

John Evans, who had been a member of the 1971 Everest rescue team, radioed from Camp I to have half-hour radio contact from five o'clock on. Probably remembering Bahuguna's plight, Evans shook me and Lou out of our complacency and got us ready to move. At 5:30, there was still no word of Kiran. We readied to descend to look for him while Jim and Peter were to climb up. We would start at 6:00 P.M. if Kiran hadn't been seen.

"I see them!" Peter yelled from below Jim's Lead. "He's with Devi and Willi below Roskelley Dump."

Several minutes later, Jim radioed to us at Camp III that Kiran was all right and coming down. The whole episode drained us all, and only confirmed our fear that Kiran's judgment was less than sound. His pride was dangerous.

During the evening radio call, Lou asked Jim to move to Camp II the next day to help work on the Buttress. Several members, including Peter and Kiran, were furious at this development. They felt they had earned the right to move up, that Jim was being given the chance because I insisted. They were right. In my opinion the Buttress was going to take a team that worked well together. Jim and I were just that pair.

Lou understood my request for Jim. The Buttress was going to need a strong team who had experience on similar terrain. Speed would be essential. Jim and I had climbed some of the most difficult routes in the Canadian Rockies together as well as a major first ascent of a technical rock-and-ice face on a 7,000-meter peak in Bolivia. Jim and I were by far the fastest, most proficient team on the mountain. We also needed results fast to keep the expedition from stalling.

The expedition was at its most difficult point. Not only did we have the Buttress to contend with, but also the many personal conflicts that seemed to get worse every day. We were going to have our hands full.

Lou and I awoke to the intense cold of 22,000 feet. Our first day would be spent descending to Roskelley Dump, sixteen hundred feet below the camp, to retrieve rope, hardware, and food for our attempt on the Buttress. We hoped the other climbers below would carry from their camps to the Ridge or to Roskelley Dump. Support from below would be vital to our success.

The descent was easy and we moved rapidly from rappel to rappel. Several rope lengths above the Dump we passed Peter, Jim, and Nirmal carrying to Camp III. They had left Camp II at 2:30 A.M. and had gained surprisingly little elevation.

Lou and I were careful not to rappel through the ascent tracks of the previous day. We moved right or left to avoid destroying any steps that would make reascending to Camp II more difficult for us and the others. No new snow had fallen during the night, although spindrift avalanches had covered some sections of rope.

At the cache, Lou grabbed three ropes and started back behind Nirmal, last of the three climbers. I loaded my pack with food and rope and followed. My job was to remove all the carabiners that had been used at anchor points and replace them with webbing. Although heavily loaded and working on the route, I passed Nirmal and caught Jim and Peter below the Ridge, and finally struggled into camp. After a few minutes' rest I descended again some six hundred feet to a belay station for a rack of pitons that had been left behind during the ascent. With the light load and excellent tracks, I broke into camp again shortly behind Nirmal.

The sun was warming the air at Camp III, so we sat comfortably in the snow to study our next problem, the Buttress. Lou and I were quiet but optimistic.

Several sections looked like a desperate struggle: blank, overhanging, and covered with a thin sheet of rime ice and powder snow. At the midway point a short steep snowfield began a series of "easier" pitches, including what appeared to be a long snow gully to just below the top of the Buttress. The difficulties ended with several hundred feet of vertical rock. The team was fully aware of its significance in determining whether the route would go. If we couldn't climb the Buttress, there would be no summit.

Peter was discouraged. "Wow! I don't know whether I can climb that," he said to Jim. "I would like to try and find a route traversing along to the left. There's got to be a large couloir on the face, according to Bonington's photo. Willi thinks traversing to the left would be a good idea, too."

Peter had thought there was a "super couloir" to the top long before we even left the United States. Bonington's photo, taken from Changabang, did suggest a possible route, but from Camp III it looked very dangerous. We argued the merits of the two routes.

"Your route, Peter, traverses directly along the breaking point for avalanches," Lou pointed out. "Even if you made it around to the left, there may not be this couloir you seem to think is there."

"The Buttress is the safest, most direct route," I added. "We'll have to give it a try first before risking your mythical couloir."

"Not everyone will be able to get up that Buttress. I want to see everyone have a chance."

"So do we, Peter. But only if it's safe."

The discussion proved pointless. Peter was determined

to give the traverse a try as soon as he moved to Camp III. He asked Lou if he could come up the next day.

"No," Lou said. "There's not enough food or equipment stocked here at Camp III yet. Everyone has to carry several loads to here before moving up."

This irritated Peter even more.

"If you guys can get to that gully two-thirds of the way up, it will probably go," Peter said. He turned, discouraged, and disappeared down the ropes to his camp.

The pressure to achieve success on the Buttress was on. Lou, Jim, and I knew if we didn't make good progress the next day, the team would demand we turn our effort to the suicidal traverse left. Peter had made it clear that the others felt we were trying a route that was too difficult for some of the team even to follow. They would not help our effort for long. Although the three of us felt that even a single man on the top was a success for all, others below felt that everyone should have an equal chance or no one should.

At 2:00 P.M. radio call, another heated discussion ensued concerning Peter's desire to move up to Camp III the next day and our decision to try the Buttress. The argument was relayed through Andy at Camp I to Peter at Camp II and back because of poor radio reception at Camp II. But Lou stood firm. No one was to move up until Camp III had been stocked and some progress had been made on the Buttress.

Matters hadn't improved at 7:00 P.M. radio call. Peter still felt he deserved to move and work on the traverse left. Then Devi's voice, broken by static, came over the radio. "Camp III, this is Camp II. Over."

I answered her call because Lou was tired of arguing.

"Kiran and I will carry to III tomorrow," she said.

Lou overheard the statement and surmised that neither Peter nor Nirmal would be carrying. He burst out of the tent in a rage and grabbed the radio.

"Is Peter going to carry with you?"

"Peter said he would take a rest day unless he could move up," Devi answered.

Lou was furious with Peter. "Everyone should carry at

least to Roskelley Dump tomorrow. That's all from Camp III."

August 26 was cold. I awoke around 5:00 A.M. Although I was toasty in my bag, the air had frosted my nose and cheeks. Where I exhaled, hoar frost clung to the small face opening of my bag. The shock of cold air in contact with warm skin was painful.

"Jim," I yelled through the dark at the other two-man tent, "better start getting ready. We've got a long day ahead."

Lou awoke to help us get ready and share in the slow preparation of breakfast. Cooking was always awkward. Before the stove was started, several potloads of snow were packed and put within easy reach; a large nylon stuff sack was packed full in case more was needed. The stove's aircraft kerosene fuel, purchased in New Delhi, fired only after a lengthy priming, then required constant vigilance to be sure only the stove was on fire. Every tent at Camp III eventually had a burn hole in the door from the stoves.

Food was stacked neatly inside the door vestibule. Everything was bagged in plastic and tied to prevent moisture from ruining anything. Although the cook had the warmest place in the tent, he also had the dirtiest, wettest, most awkward job. Compliments to the chef were the only reward:

"This stuff tastes like shit!"

"Wake up! You're burning the tent door!"

"Goddamn it, Roskelley! You spilled sugar all over my bag!"

Amen.

Jim and I were soon ready. We had gathered the necessary ropes, pitons, webbing, ice axes, hammers, and personal gear the night before into our packs and now added only lunch, water, and clothing. The loads were heavy.

Clouds began drifting in from the south as we post-holed to our thighs in the crusted snow along the Ridge crest. Slowly we neared the Buttress—less than half a mile from Camp III. Stopping briefly, I removed my boots and rubbed some feeling back into my numb toes. I had lost some toes on Dhaulagiri in 1973 and didn't intend to lose any more. Jim surveyed our intended route while stamping his own feet to regain circulation. We moved on.

"This is where we should rope up and start fixing, Jim." We were at a sharp crest directly underneath the first rock outcrop that looked difficult. The Northwest Face dropped away for thousands of feet while the Northeast Face angled at sixty degrees. It dropped in a broken mass at the Northeast Glacier.

Directly above, our Buttress rose vertically. The pink-red quartzite was draped in a fine layer of fresh powder snow. From below we could see few decent belay ledges. Several bands of rock were overhanging for some distance; obviously, they were very technical sections.

I was ready within a few minutes and waded to the rock outcrop, using my arms like paddles to move up and across to an area of broken rock.

"Ready Jim?" I watched him finish tying the knot to his swami belt.

He grabbed my belay line and sat down. "Go ahead."

Driving my ice axe into a crack for support, I muscled onto a narrow ledge. Several feet higher, a fist crack enabled me to reach a steep narrow snow ramp that traversed to a short snowfield. I followed a crest through waist-deep sugar snow 150 feet to the start of the Buttress proper. A bombproof belay ended the first 250 feet of climbing.

"O.K. Jim, you're tied off!"

I stamped out a one-foot-square stance while watching Jim attach his jumars and ascend until out of sight below the rock outcrop. It seemed ages until he appeared on the edge of the snowfield.

"My jumar system is all fouled up," he yelled, visibly exhausted. "I'll be up as soon as I fix it." I was becoming very impatient.

"Damn, I got hung up on the rock and the rope got caught in the crack," he said. "I never struggled so hard in my life." Jim had a monstrous load of rope and hardware, and jumaring on this low-angled ground had proven almost impossible. As Jim tied in and became comfortable, I handed him my end to another three hundred feet of nine-millimeter rope with which to belay me. The next section of rock looked extremely difficult.

Everything had a fine layer of sugar snow covering it and the snow had to be removed before I could move. I climbed delicately, clearing the snow from each foot and handhold to be sure of its stability. The rock was blocky; holds were scattered and small. I mantled three large blocks before being forced to traverse to my left by a blank band. The route was to the right, so after placing a shaky piton, I moved toward a shallow chimney eighty feet directly above Jim's belay and back on route. Knocking in several pitons, I asked Jim to move up to my position because I couldn't be sure where the next belay would be.

He got his jumar system working right and despite his heavy load, ascended quickly. As soon as he was set, I was off once more into the gully. Using a small hold inside and bridging with my feet against the two walls, I gained another seventy-five feet to a pedestal. Again, I couldn't see anything but vertical walls above, so I banged in several belay pitons and tied Jim off. The pitch could have been the "exit cracks" on the Eiger North Wall.

We were moving smoothly now. Periodic spindrift avalanches rained down upon us, but we seemed to be out of the main avalanches on either side. The route was proving to be safe. The clear skies of morning had turned into a thick, billowing gray and snow began to fall.

"Good lead, John. How are you doing?"

"Cold, but I think it's going to go. Belay on?"

Jim readied himself, while I looked for some alternative to the vertical wall. Everywhere the rock walls seemed blank, vertical, or slightly overhanging.

"Keep the rope tight while I drop down and see what's around this corner."

I down-climbed several feet below the pedestal, spread-eagled across a gap, and grabbed a good hold on the outward-tilting wall. The traverse looked thin, a three-foot-wide slope of seventy-degree ice on a narrow ledge, but the wall above had small holds for my hands. Once around the corner I disappeared from sight and communication became difficult. The wall bulged, forcing me to lean out backwards while attempting to kick steps in the snow. Both Jim and I were carrying fifty-pound loads of rope and hardware; their weight pulled us out from the wall on the traverse. After thirty feet the traverse ended in a short ledge system below two overhanging walls at ninety degrees to each other. One wall was split with a vertical crack that looked hand-and-fist size.

"Jim! Hey, Jim!" I screamed for him to hear me. "I'm going to try a crack above me. Got a good belay?" I wanted him to dig in deeper if he wasn't already badger tight.

His reply was barely audible behind the walls. "O.K.!"

I prepared for the worst. After placing a good pin, I removed my pack, retrieved my etriers, and hooked them where they could be reached easily if I needed them. Strapping my ice axe to my waist and putting my pack back on, I began jamming the overhanging fist crack. I was not wearing gloves and my hands froze instantly. After I gained twenty feet to a point where the wall overhung, I could find no more toe holds for the front points of my crampons. The crack was choked with ice.

Hanging on one jammed fist, I reached for a two-and-a-half-inch bong piton and placed it in the crack two feet above. My parka hid my hammer, which became entangled as I tried to free it from the holster. Finally I drove the bong deep, clipped in a carabiner and an etrier, and somehow got my cramponed boot into the lower step. I was almost done in.

I pulled for slack to put it through the carabiner, then relaxed. My hands were numb. I warmed them with my breath until they began to tingle and ache, then slipped my gloves back on.

Two more pins brought me to the lip of the wall. I couldn't seem to make the transition from vertical to the easy slope above because there was nothing but sugar snow to hold onto. After the traverse and tight corners, the drag from the rope had become a tug-of-war and hindered me from making any type of move.

Swinging my left leg up and over to the top of the other wall, I crab-crawled over to its top, pulled for some slack, and finally stood up. I was on a sixty-degree slope that led through several rock steps to the base of an overhanging band of bright red quartzite.

I waded forward, stopping to yank violently at the rope every few feet for more slack, then moved on. Surmounting the few rock steps was not difficult, and within a half hour I reached the base of the red wall.

The weather had worsened during my battle with the crack below and now it was snowing and blowing steadily. I knocked in several pins and tied off.

"Jim!" I yelled. He couldn't hear me. "Jim! You're tied off!" We were too far apart and out of sight of each other. I glanced at my watch. It was already 4:00 P.M.

Leaving the extra rope and hardware, I rappeled to the lip of the overhang, pulled as much slack as possible, and dropped over the side, cleaning the pins as I rappeled. My ice axe caught on the lip and stabbed me in the gut part way over. The traverse was dangerous and strenuous to retrace. I had to rappel sideways while climbing back to Jim. A slip would have swung me across and down to the black and overhanging Northwest Face.

Jim was ghostly white. His beard and moustache were solid ice and he must have frozen waiting for me, but his concern was for me and the route. "What did it look like above?"

"I reached that band of overhanging red rock. It's going to be difficult, but I saw a break in it just above the belay. I bet you're frozen."

"I'll be O.K. Do you want a bite to eat?"

"No, let's get our asses off this thing and eat below."

A half hour later we were at the beginning of the fixed lines. Only then did we realize we were exhausted. We had been moving hard since 7:00 A.M. and it was now 5:00 P.M. With effort, we removed our crampons and opened a can of chicken spread. It had been a cold, windy day and we still had the trudge through the packed snow back to Camp III.

Refortified and pleased with our effort, we turned for camp to tell the others the good news. The Buttress would go.

ELEVEN

Back at Camp III, Lou had been busy during the day. He had descended to Roskelley Dump that morning to carry gear back up. He waited for some time at the cache, but no one from below was carrying. In anger, he loaded two food bags, each weighing over thirty pounds, into his pack and returned to Camp III. Something was wrong below. He would find out at the 2:00 P.M. radio call.

"Camp One, Camp One, come in," Lou recited. "This is Camp Three."

"Afternoon, Lou," Willi replied. "How's everything up above?"

"John and Jim made good progress up the Buttress, Willi, but it looks like slow, difficult work from here. Everybody O.K. down there? No one carried to Roskelley Dump."

Willi explained that instead of carrying, those at Camp II had descended to Camp I at Pete's urging to discuss the alternate route and Lou's decision to bring Jim up to Camp III. "We felt the day would be better spent discussing the route and the goals of the expedition members here, Lou," continued Willi. "Down here we feel that if it means getting a few climbers to the summit up the Buttress, or most of us up an easier route to the left, we'd rather explore the alternate route."

"They're doing better than even I'd have imagined on the Buttress," Lou repeated. "Besides, if you're talking about Peter's route to the left, it should be considered only as a last resort because of avalanche danger."

"Peter has great reservations about letting John and Jim

on the Buttress. And I think you're losing control of John and Jim—your common sense is being overridden by their enthusiasm."

"He's just jealous, Willi."

"Maybe," Willi came back, "but he also thinks the route on the left exists and will enable more of us to reach the summit. Peter wants the chance to come up and explore his ideas."

"Peter's attitude really angers me, Willi. He's made fewer carries than anyone on the team and I don't like being told that he would carry today only if he could move up. Devi has carried and contributed far more. *She* should move up before Peter. I had originally planned for her to climb with John, but she had that sore throat.

"We came to climb the North Ridge," Lou continued, "and all my actions are directed toward getting as many people up it as possible."

"Well, Lou, I don't know what's going to happen now. We'll discuss your decision down here and get back to you. I can't promise you Peter will continue to climb. Just don't let John and Jim talk you into the wrong decisions for the whole team."

"We have no enthusiasm for Peter's route—it's an avalanche trap! If that route would go, it'd be alpine style with just a few climbers—only a few would make the top. The crux of the Buttress route is the first six hundred feet. Once we're past that, the climbing will ease up. It looks like a gully for the last four or five hundred feet."

"We're patient. Once you guys are through, our group will give the route to the left a try."

"Plan what you want, Willi. Can I count on someone bringing more rope up to the dump in the morning?"

"We'll talk at six o'clock. I can't promise anything now."

It was then Lou realized he was becoming a "bad guy" because he wanted a decision on the Buttress first, not a split route. Clearly some of those below hoped the Buttress attempt would fail and an easier route found; they doubted they could get up the Buttress even by jumaring.

Jim and I arrived in camp just as Lou made the 6:00 P.M. radio call. We could overhear the tense conversation with those below. After dumping my pack I walked over to Lou, who handed me the radio in disgust.

"Here, tell them what it's like on the Buttress. They're determined to go around left."

I explained to Willi the climbing we had done that day. "It'll go, Willi, but the fewer people on the ropes the better—those nine-millimeters are going to fray on that sharp rock. It's too dangerous for more than a team of two to be working on it. Rockfall would be bad."

"Well, we're going to give the traverse route to the left a try while you're plugging away on the Buttress," Willi said. "Peter wants to move up and work on that route."

Willi's insistence on sending Peter up infuriated me. "As far as I'm concerned," I stated flatly, "if Peter doesn't want to carry, tell him to go home."

Willi said quietly he would pass on my message and we ended the contact. It had gone poorly and I had lost my temper. Again we were divided into two groups. I had been hard on Peter, but I felt he was instigating the dissension. Only John Evans, who was at Camp I with Willi and knew little of the problems being discussed, was able to distance himself from the disagreements.

Lou, Jim, and I talked out the situation over dinner at Camp III, but in our righteous state of mind we did little to solve the problem. We were disgusted that the others were considering giving up the original plans because not everyone would summit on the Buttress route. Let them go left. We would continue climbing on the Buttress until we made it. In our opinion it was climbable and the only safe route.

I didn't want to leave the tent on the morning of the twenty-seventh. Lou was rustling about, dressing, and I was procrastinating, hoping the weather was too fierce to climb. Jim and I eventually dressed, made breakfast, and crawled from our tents. Neither of us wanted to admit we didn't want to go; we reluctantly loaded more ropes into our packs and set off along the Ridge at 8:30 A.M.

I didn't feel strong enough to break trail, but managed for half the distance before turning the miserable job over to Jim. We said little as we plugged along, punching through the wind-blown crust. Every so often we would stop to rest and I would search Jim's face for any hint to return to camp. His mirrored sunglasses hid any feelings he had. We reached the fixed lines not really thinking we would go up, but without stopping I got out my jumars and etriers, fastened them to the line and jumared into the howling wind and blowing snow. I knew Jim would follow.

The second fixed rope scared me. Fifty feet above, the rope ran over a knife-sharp edge of rock. As I began jumaring, the rope stretched and the rock seemed to saw right through it. I couldn't move the rope to either side. Easing my weight up, I tried not to bounce as I ascended. The rope severed in half a thousand times in my mind before I passed the frayed section. Once finished, I moved the rope to the side to protect Jim.

The rest of the jumar to the end of our first day's climb was just as scary. I made the traverse of the previous day to the jam crack and waited in my harness for Jim so I could yell instructions to him. When I reached the snowfield above I flung the rope over to the pedestal. This erased the difficult traverse and made the ascent easier and safer. I busied myself at our high point arranging the hardware and ropes. Jim arrived exhausted, warm from the exertion. Spindrift blew into our eyes, noses, and clothing. We couldn't tell if it was snowing or the wind was just blowing old snow around us. After a while it didn't matter.

All the preparation of setting up a workable belay was in vain as I hooked up my belay line incorrectly, tangled the ropes, and had to step over Jim to get free. I began the pitch by descending and moving to my right over seventy-degree rock slabs covered with sugar snow. I feared the entire slab would break loose each time I moved. Thirty feet up I reached the bottom of the band and traversed left to a break through the overhanging wall. A bulging off-width chimney looked like the only way.

I fiddled with bongs (two- to four-inch aluminum pitons), then blades (thin steel pitons), sunk back into the back of the chimney, but nothing seemed to work. Climbing into the chimney itself, I reached a large block with a thin crack and drove in a knife-blade piton the thickness of a razor. I was finally protected.

My etriers caught on my crampons as I pulled them to the pin. I struggled desperately to hold on and free them, meanwhile catching my ice axe, which was hanging from my belt, under my foot. Once free of the hangups, I got into the etriers and stood up. The bulge, compounded by the heavy load in my pack, was pushing me out. I slammed in a good angle piton and repeated my performance, complete with my ice axe tying up my legs and holding me until I was exhausted.

One more piton and I was able to mantle to the top of the chimney. I grabbed a two-foot-square boulder for support but was startled when it came with me. I froze, then put the rock back in place; the block would have flattened Jim, who was standing fifty feet directly below. He was already having to eat more than his share of the garbage that I was kicking down on him.

Jim's position often seemed more frightening to me than leading a difficult stretch of ground. His stance, often small and uncomfortable, was usually directly underneath me. He had full view of the twenty-four sharp points on my crampons as I climbed above him. These, and the needle-sharp points of my ice tools, would be lethal weapons if I were to fall. Although I tried not to kick snow and rocks down on him, there was a constant barrage of debris that I couldn't help but dislodge along with the snow that I had to deliberately clear away before each move. He must have been frozen during several long belays, but did not complain. I couldn't have wished for a better partner to second me.

From the top of the mantle I flailed away at the icy crust that covered a sloping one-foot ledge I needed to traverse. If someone had watched this desperate action, he would have thought I was trying to kill Jim with ice and rock. But it was our only choice.

Tiptoeing left for twenty feet positioned me in a small gully where the garbage I was kicking down fell away from Jim's position. Meanwhile, I was caught in a major spindrift avalanche zone that emptied a snowfield one hundred feet above. Every thirty seconds I was hit by a mass of snow. The wall above was broken, but vertical. How was I going to climb it while being bombarded by constant avalanches? The rope drag was terrible at this point as well. I hammered in two good pins, tied off, and yelled for Jim to come up.

While waiting, I managed to kick out a place for my right foot and put the left on a small rock for my stance. Forty-five minutes later Jim appeared over the overhang, barely visible through the spindrift and blowing snow. I argued with myself on what to do next.

Could we continue under such adverse conditions? I was freezing from inaction and Jim was faring no better. He followed the rope along the traverse, leaving in one pin in case someone should slip off and not be able to get back on. As he approached, a horrendous avalanche dropped upon us: Jim drifted in and out of sight although he was only fifteen feet away. The situation was so severe it was funny. Jim came out of it laughing. When he reached me, we laughed for some time as each avalanche hit us and sloughed off.

"What do you think, John? Do we rap off?"

"Let's give it five minutes. It's only two o'clock. If the avalanches quit, I'll give the next pitch a try."

Jim leaned over toward me as I lifted another coil of rope from his pack and we began to unravel the three-hundred-foot mess. He reached my water bottle and we each took our first swig of the day. We were hungry, but too cold to look for food, unwrap it, and eat.

As if the Goddess Nanda Devi heard us, the avalanches stopped. The sun's rays filtered through the billowing clouds, brightening our precarious little stance. I started one more pitch.

The rope was still like tangled spaghetti, but we unraveled enough for me to start. Jim pulled back his hood so he could watch carefully, ready for a fall. I inched up a slabby corner to a small overhang. Difficult chimneying took me to a small stance. Avalanches started again but I decided not to stop.

A thin crack led back right over Jim, and I worked my way up on pitons to several upside-down blocks. Several more loose pins and I had gained another thin, awkward stance. For climbing, gloves were useless but I did put them on at each stance to rewarm my frozen fingers. Avalanches streamed down the route, burying Jim and me for minutes at a time, threatening to sweep me off.

I had no choice but to free-climb the remainder of the wall. It was the most difficult mixed climbing I had ever encountered; pins were useless for protection in the loose blocks that were frozen in place, and my weight cracked them loose with each move. A tiny flake for one of my crampon points and a fingerhold kept me attached while I chopped away the layer of crusty snow. I found a cold hand-jam and hung on long enough to slam in a horizontal piton, sling it, and ready myself for the next move.

There seemed to be no handholds ahead, so I stepped up carefully while pulling down on the sling. Twenty pounds of rock moved with it. Luckily, I hadn't pulled straight out. I was out of carabiners. There were no more holds. I stuck the shaft of my axe in some spindrift crust at arm's length, tested slightly, and pulled down on it enough to muscle up on my left leg. I stepped cautiously onto sixty-degree sugar snow on smooth slab. There was no place to stand. Without putting my 145 pounds at any one place all at once, I maneuvered to a pedestal forty feet up. I was stuck again. The snowfield we had been hoping to reach was only six feet away but there were no holds or cracks.

I mantled, pulling up with my arms with every ounce of energy I had left until my crampons were level with my hands. There were no holds, only bottomless sugar snow. I balanced for several seconds, then placed my weight onto one foot. It stayed long enough for me to wade upward several feet and away from the lip of the wall. After swimming through sixty feet of waist-deep avalanche snow, I finally smacked in a bombproof angle piton.

It was late and again I couldn't hear Jim. I had taken more than an hour on the long pitch, so I secured the line to several pins, attached my rappel system and, cleaning the pins as I went, descended in the blinding snowstorm. Jim was waiting patiently, stamping his feet and slapping his hands for warmth, hiding beneath a small overhang and his pack.

A rainbow appeared through the thick clouds and, for a split second, the snow-covered peaks stood out boldly in the distance. The rappels in the storm were frightening but dramatically beautiful. But we desperately needed eleven-millimeter rope to replace the already fraying nine-millimeter; the ropes ran over countless edges of rock resembling broken glass. We hoped the sahibs below had carried drops to the cache for Lou to bring to Camp III.

On the pedestal, two rappels from the Ridge, I attached my rappel system to the rope and waited for Jim. He appeared directly above and lowered beside me.

"I'll see you at the bottom," I said.

"Say, use my camera and take a picture of me, will you?"

"Sure."

I began to wrap the rappel rope around my leg so I could free my hands. Only there was no rope, just twenty feet of tail. I had clipped onto the wrong rope. I was attached to a short section of leftover rope that hung over the Northwest Face.

I felt nauseous at the thought of what could have happened—plummeting thousands of vertical feet down the Northwest Face to eventually hit the glacier and sweep past Advanced Base for the Rishi ten thousand feet below. Dumbfounded, neither of us spoke but looked at each other with equally shocked expressions. How had I made that mistake? Exhaustion? One thing was certain: we would have to be extra careful from now on.

We reached the Ridge without further incident. I was still shaking from my close call. Rappeling has always been considered the most dangerous part of mountaineering. I had known climbers who rappeled off the end of their rappel line, but I had never been that close before.

As dusk turned the mountain into shadow, Lou was on the radio when we struggled into camp. His conversation was heated. Again, no one had carried from Camp II and Lou was disgusted. Even worse, we were running short of rope for the Buttress and needed several lengths of eleven-millimeter to make the climbing safer.

"I've got some bad news for you Lou," Willi reported. "Peter has decided to descend and quit the mountain. Nirmal is on the verge of the same thing. Your insistence on keeping John and Jim on the Buttress is creating real problems down here."

Nirmal, disgusted with Himalayan climbing and the continual problems, decided this was his last expedition and descended to Camp I. Annoyed that I had told him to leave the mountain, Peter also descended to Camp I. He intended to leave. Andy moved from Camp I up to Camp II to take Peter's place. Only the porters at Advanced Base had carried, and only to Camp I.

"Well, they can't continue on the Buttress with no rope and I didn't see anyone carrying up to the dump again today," Lou snapped. "We need rope, Willi. At least have someone bring it up."

"My hands are tied. You've made it hard for me just to keep people here on the mountain. What are you going to do when John and Jim reach Camp Four, pull them off? We took a vote down here and decided the first team to the summit should be you and Devi."

Lou replied with caution. "I'm very honored, but I would never pull Jim and John off after doing such a great job. I'd always planned to join them . . . perhaps Devi could join us also? I see nothing wrong with a foursome."

The conversation had been a touchy one, but Lou had handled it with great tact, even though he was irritated with the decisions being made below.

Jim and I had to laugh at the other climbers' sudden change of commitment—from trying the mythical route to the left to the now surer success up the fixed lines of the Buttress. Lou had told Willi in his first reports how we were nearing the gully two-thirds of the way and that it looked easier from that point on. This changed the situation completely for the others. What alarmed us was their desire to place Devi so high on the mountain without having her acclimatize by carrying and living higher.

Lou told us what to expect. "Devi, Kiran, or Nirmal

will move up tomorrow, according to Willi. I requested a minimum of two ropes to Camp Three and two more at Roskelley Dump. I also asked for four tents, two for Camp Four and two for here. Willi promised they would be there.''

At Camp III, Jim, Lou, and I tried to discuss only the Buttress and the route, but our conversation kept returning to the problems of the team. We needed teamwork if we were to summit, yet the two factions were getting further apart physically and idealogically. Nothing was certain. We still had to surmount the Buttress, place a camp up high, and make a summit bid. Those were problems enough without this split in the team.

Jim and I rested on August 28. Exhausted mentally and physically, we needed to regain our strength after our desperate climbing for the past two days between 23,000 and 24,000 feet. Lou decided to descend to Roskelley Dump for a load and left early, hoping to get back to camp before the sun came up.

Most of the team was moving to one camp or another that morning and we were expecting Devi, Andy, Nirmal, and Kiran at Camp III. Lou had argued against anyone moving up until more loads had been carried to Camp III, but his explanations had fallen on deaf ears. Camp III was going to be a bottleneck of climbers with no food, tents, or equipment.

As Jim and I finished a late breakfast, Peter staggered into camp carrying a light load from Camp I. Heading straight for me, he was obviously there for a specific purpose.

"I want to talk with you John,'' Peter said. I was immediately on the defense.

"I'm really pissed that you think you have the right to tell me to go home. I've been trying to do my job as well as any of you and what you've done on this climb doesn't give you the right to order me or anyone around. Lou told me you didn't want me on the Buttress. Why?''

I was surprised Peter had come all the way from Camp I to confront me with this. When I realized he hadn't even carried a load to supply us, I was angry.

"I don't care for your ways, Peter. Know why? Because you won't carry loads except when you want. Because you insist on following through on ideas when you've been asked not to. Because you want to move to higher camps without carrying or acclimatizing. Then, when you don't get your way, you descend and cause a rift in the team!"

We argued back and forth for some time. Jim kept out of the discussion.

"You told us you didn't want to work on the Buttress," I continued. "Jim and I are moving at a good clip and we should have it done in one more day. The ropes are fraying terribly and the fewer people on them the safer they'll be—that's why Lou hasn't been going up. The most important thing now is to get the equipment to us so we can continue working on it. No one except Lou has carried for several days. What kind of teamwork is that? You wanted to go left around the Buttress because you didn't think everyone could get up it even when it got fixed with rope."

Lou arrived as our argument ended. He was Peter's next target.

"Lou, there's been an empty space in one of the tents up here and I want to know why you haven't given it to me," he demanded. "I feel good and I'll be a judge of my own health."

"Lou was voted by everyone as the climbing leader, Peter," I said, jumping to Lou's defense. "Whatever his reasons, he is trying to be fair. There are several climbers below who have carried much more than you and deserve to come up first, but the camp isn't ready logistically. There's not even enough food, gas, or tents here yet."

Peter acknowledged the problem Lou had been facing as climbing leader: trying to keep the route progressing while keeping the sahibs below carrying gear up the mountain to supply those above. And from our camp now, Peter could see the top of our ropes on the Buttress. This alone was enough to make him realize our chances of success were good—for the expedition, for everyone. The route to the left was put aside, and Peter left Camp III with a better understanding. I was later glad that Peter had taken the initiative to confront us with his feelings. It was a relief to have had the issues discussed in the open. As the argument had progressed, I could see the cause of the team's problems: no communication.

Soon after Lou arrived, Devi and Andy came into camp. There were no extra tents, so they moved in with Jim. He wasn't pleased with the crowded conditions, especially when this was one of the reasons no one should have moved up. Nirmal and Kiran were the next to arrive, bringing with them another two-man tent. While Devi and Andy cooked dinner for seven, the rest of us helped dig a platform and pitch the tent for the Indians.

We crammed five into one tent to eat and passed food to Kiran and Nirmal several feet away. Everyone was uncomfortable, but it proved easier than passing food from tent to tent. The effort of trying to eat crammed into a small corner with my legs tucked under me was too much and I finally crawled back to my own tent for the night.

Blasts of wind against the tent woke me at 5:00 A.M. Hoar frost, shaken off the tent ceiling, had soaked the tops of our bags and frozen into stiff white sheets.

"Hey, Jim!" I yelled. "What do you think we ought to do?"

"It's awfully windy, but we could at least go to the base," he replied. Lou agreed. He would go with us to help double some of the badly frayed fixed lines.

Out of the tent and into the cold wind was just the beginning to a long day. I took the lead up the Ridge, slowly breaking trail, stumbling in the deep wind-packed crust. Pausing after each step, we moved along like three spacemen. The wind cut through our face openings and found the weaknesses in our clothing. No one spoke, only nodded or pointed. That morning we all wondered why we were moving instead of hiding from the storm.

Lou relieved me at the halfway point and continued breaking to the base of the Buttress. The bottoms of my feet ached from a deep, numbing cold as though I had frostbite again. Each time I sat down, I held them out of the snow and beat them together to restore my poor circulation. The weather was bad.

At the Buttress I began the long and dangerous jumar to Sugar Delight Snowfield, the name I had given the high point I reached two days before. Each rope stretched like a rubber band before it pulled taut, took my weight, and let me inch upward. The rope had frayed severely in spots from even the few times Jim and I had jumared and rappeled. The sight of the white core of the rope exposed through the frayed sheath stretching over knife-edged rocks gave me a queasy feeling. We definitely needed to double the lines.

Jim started immediately after me, but soon fell far behind. I reached Sugar Delight Snowfield and the top of the ropes at eleven o'clock, sat down, and waited. Around noon Jim poked his head over the edge, then threw his body and load onto the snowfield. He was exhausted.

"Where's Lou?"

"He's doubling two ropes down below," Jim replied. "I don't know whether he's going to come up all the way with us or not."

"I hope so—we've got only two ropes and we're going to need a third today."

We opened a can of chicken spread for lunch, then I disappeared down several feet and traversed right through waist-deep snow onto a steep hundred-foot hidden chimney to our right. My ice axe proved to be the only hold and it was shaky at best. I climbed to the top of the chimney, which left me straddling a ten-foot crest that dropped off hundreds of feet on either side and butted up against a blank wall.

The gully we hoped to reach was forty feet to my right and definitely difficult to get to. By its looks, the gully would be easy for some four hundred feet. Lou yelled from below and I turned to see his cap appear at the edge of Sugar Delight. We would have the rope.

I noticed a foot-wide ledge running the length of the wall that blocked my way to the gully. Bashing in a knife-blade piton for protection, I lowered myself, hanging from my hands on the ledge. I moved hand over hand the thirty feet of ledge to just above an easy drop to the gully, placed another pin, and lowered myself to the ice below.

The fury of the storm increased and the spindrift

avalanches at Sugar Delight seemed small compared to the steady, knee-deep avalanche that was running down the gully. It was clear this was how the gully had formed.

I was completely out of earshot of Jim; the rope, wrapped over and around the corner I had climbed, had me pulling like a draft horse. I had to reach a descent belay. The gully was deep, the left wall was 175 feet high and the right rose hundreds of feet to the top of the Buttress. Both were vertical. I had no choice but to ascend the gully to its top, some four hundred feet up. A difficult ice-and-rock section took me fifteen minutes to surmount on my way to what appeared to be a protected belay fifty feet from my landing point. The rope drag almost stopped me.

When I stopped, I was three hundred feet out from Jim and slightly above the avalanches in the gully. The little stance was perfect and had several cracks in which to place bombproof pins. I finally tied off the rope and yelled for Jim to follow. It was useless. In the storm, it was like a bullhorn trying to attract the attention of a deaf mute and neither one understanding the other. But, as if he could read by mind, Jim came anyway.

Jim had taken off his crampons and managed the chimney and traverse only with great difficulty. The drop into the gully took him valuable minutes, but he finally arrived fifty feet below me. He totally exhausted himself climbing up the steep icy section to my belay.

"Lou's coming just behind me. He's bringing another rope."

"I'll lead this gully because I'm rested. As soon as you see me wave at the top, start up. You'll be tied off."

I grabbed the three hundred feet of rope from Jim's pack, uncoiled it, tied it to me, and started climbing. It caught below, but Jim managed to free it as I punched my way through the deep snow on the right side of the gully. It was slow, exhausting work. Sometimes I waded waist deep and was completely stopped until I could grab a hold alongside the rock wall and pull myself forward a few feet to easier ground. The snow was bottomless. An overhanging chockstone was the last obstacle and I was able to chimney and jam its left corner to surmount it.

Thirty feet more and I straddled a knife-bladed crest and the end of the gully.

I searched fruitlessly for a decent crack to tie the rope to, but finally settled on a thin blade driven in horizontally. I waved down to Jim.

Lou had reached Jim's side and now they both clipped to the rope and came together. They were having a difficult time without crampons. Slowly they waded to their waists, then slipped back. I was glad they didn't know how poor the anchor was.

They reached the overhanging chockstone and I watched as Lou's head appeared over the edge, then disappeared back down. Again he appeared, struggling to get his jumar over the lip, but failed and fell back to Jim below. He straightened out the problem with Jim, who had been pulling on the rope and not giving him any slack. He finally came over the top and dropped into the snow, exhausted. After recovering, Lou climbed to my small stance, followed closely by Jim.

Jim's conversation and speech were difficult to understand. His attention seemed far away. I worried about his control.

Lou didn't speak, but took the rope and gazed at me dully, then at the wall above us. I moved back along the crest to get a better look at the problem. There was not much to go on, but I thought a traverse left should be tried first.

I felt confident and strong, even though I was cold and it was 4:45 P.M. The pitch would have to be done quickly. I traversed left across a seventy-five-degree ice slope to ice-covered rock. Mantle after mantle for forty feet brought me to a stance and I stopped. There were no cracks with which to protect myself, but the rock was ledgy and I didn't feel that any one move as yet had been dangerous. I inched back to beneath several overhangs that looked difficult to bypass and paused to place a shaky pin in a rotten crack. This gave me the courage to move up on loose blocks covered with crusty snow. There weren't any good holds for another fifty feet, but I worked with finesse and leg muscles, chimneying and mantling. I hacked small holds in the ice with my hammer when nothing else was there. With a bombproof knife-blade piton, I chimney-stemmed across to a one-foot-square platform on a snow rib coming from the crest above, but it was a dead end. With extreme difficulty, I climbed up and left into a vertical snow chimney and managed to place another pin in a block alongside me. There were only seventy feet to go.

Digging and clawing away the snow, I inched forward by finding holds buried deep beneath the snow chimney. I stemmed out of this after twenty feet and was on another seventy-five-degree slope, but it was loose, unconsolidated snow. After each swimming motion with my hands, I thrust the shaft of my ice axe as deep as possible and pulled until I could get solid footing below. After fifty feet of swimming I pulled myself onto the relatively flat slope of the top of the Buttress. We were there!

I hammered several good pins into a large rock outcrop twenty feet from the crest. I left the rest of the hardware attached to the anchor, fastened my rappel system to the rope, and descended, cleaning the pins as I went. It was 5:30 P.M. and too late to waste time.

The two-hundred-foot rappel went quickly and soon I was beside Lou. He immediately descended into the darkening gully. My sweat began to freeze while I waited for him to finish the rappel so I could descend. It seemed like hours.

At each rappel station, I caught Lou and had to wait. He was being cautious, but I was freezing for it. The last two rappels were doubled ropes, giving us much-needed security to the bottom.

At the base, Jim congratulated me with a big hug. He then descended slowly, fearful he would make a mistake.

We were all excited, but near to total exhaustion. After removing our climbing gear while watching a crimson sunset, we trudged wearily back to camp in the dark.

Weakened by the altitude, no one had moved from Camp III all day. Their move to Camp III the day before had only wasted food, and had not produced any loads. Peter had moved up from Camp II as well, but we remained short on gas, tents, and food. Willi, John Evans, and several porters were still below carrying loads to Roskelley Dump, but no one from Camp III was descending to pick them up. The situation was becoming critical.

Lou announced his decision that night that he, Jim, and I would make the first summit attempt after a rest day. The others said little about the decision. We ate a good meal and turned in.

We slept the next morning. Again, no one planned to descend. Devi, Andy, and Peter stayed in their tent, ate, and slept. Around 10:00 A.M. Nirmal and Kiran dressed and decided to descend for loads. Lou gave them a list of needed supplies supposedly at the cache.

Nirmal started down, leaving Kiran, who had a headache, to decide whether to attempt to carry. Jim finally convinced him not to bother. Lou questioned Peter, Devi, and Andy about their decision not to carry, but decided not to push the sensitive issue. Jim and I told them they should feel guilty watching Nirmal carry and not expecting to themselves. There was no love lost between our two tents.

It seemed like a day for petty grievances. The small, inconsequential problems were growing with the stress and altitude. The next issue was sugar. Peter wanted some in his tea that night while the rest of us wanted it for cereal in the morning. There wasn't enough for both. I longed to get away from Camp III.

Jim, Lou, and I loaded our packs that afternoon with more than seventy-five pounds of gear each. We wanted to carry only once up the frayed and dangerous ropes to Camp IV, at the top of the Buttress. The loads would be heavy but it beat climbing the ropes twice. We bedded down knowing the next few days would determine the outcome of the expedition. We had come too far, through too much, not to give it everything.

TWELVE

On the Ridge crest, gusts of wind continued to bury the already entrenched tents with snow. Jim soon had a boiling pan of jello prepared while I mixed the hot cereal for breakfast. We needed to get an early start to reach the top of the Buttress. The other climbers in camp had volunteered to break trail for us to its base. Peter left first, punching through the wind-pack to his knees. Andy and Devi followed closely. The day had fine possibilities despite the wind.

My muscles seemed unusually fatigued under the heavy load, but once I warmed up I kept a steady pace and soon overtook Andy and Devi. I followed Peter to the base of the Buttress.

Jim was tense and preoccupied with the thought of what we expected of him during the next few days. Lou and I had experienced this pressure on other trips and were, perhaps, slightly less anxious. Lou was having difficulties of another sort. Kiran insisted on carrying Lou's pack for him in an attempt to help, but the Indian's pace was much too slow. Lou diplomatically rescued his pack from Kiran part way along the Ridge to keep from falling far behind us.

I began the awesome job of jumaring to the top of the Buttress. The second lead, a slightly vertical overhanging section, proved extremely difficult to surmount with the load. I hooked the pack strap to the top jumar and slowly worked my way upward. Peter followed a short distance behind to fix the stronger eleven-millimeter ropes on the route's worst sections.

I noticed the rope had worn to the core beneath the overhanging red rock, and glared white against the dark blue sheath even from fifty feet away. My eyes never left that white core; the sharp overhang cut it even more as I jumared. It seemed like hours before I was up and over the exposed core. Once past it, I tied an overhand knot to take the tension off the cut and to protect the others as they ascended. The next length was easier and I arrived at the top of Sugar Delight Snowfield at 12:40 P.M. I decided to wait there for Jim and Lou in case they were too slow to go farther that day.

Peter arrived at my small stance an hour later. We were quiet at first, then Peter broke the silence. "John, I'm totally with the route now . . . I want you to know that."

"That's sort of a switch, isn't it? I've always had the impression you didn't care for the route."

Peter paused. "This was supposed to be a relaxed trip, John," he replied thoughtfully. "I came to be with Marty, to enjoy the mountains. That's not the way it's been. I have to admit I've been dragging my feet all the way up the mountain. That's because I felt that you, Lou, and Jim pushed the climb into something not everyone can enjoy."

"Then why was this route chosen in the first place if you all wanted a mellow trip? No one except you said a word earlier about another route."

"Lou said that you didn't want me along on the first ascent team. Why not?"

"That wasn't my decision, Peter. All I know is you've hardly carried any loads and you're not acclimatized. You just got through telling me you've been dragging your feet all the way up and now you ask me why you're not going with us?"

"I'd like to be going, John, but . . . well, good luck anyway."

"Thanks, Peter. We're hoping to make the top of the Buttress today. That way the gear will at least be there so someone—probably you—will have an easier time of it."

Jim appeared at three o'clock, in white from head to toe because of spindrift avalanches. The weather had deteriorated since morning. "Lou said to wait here," he yelled. "He's coming behind me slowly, but he thinks we won't make it today at this rate. I think he wants to go down and try again tomorrow."

Lou had expressed this doubt to Jim at the base of the Buttress that morning. He said then we were too late to start. Jim had continued up after me anyway.

"Shall we go, Lou?" I yelled.

"Yeah . . . Why not?" he yelled back.

"Follow as fast as you can," I said to Jim. "We'll never make it before dark unless we hustle."

I jamared into the snowstorm. Peter waited patiently while Jim and Lou followed to Sugar Delight Ledge. I was long gone up the ropes when Peter turned to go back to Camp III.

I felt pressured to move fast and within an hour I was at the top of the gully, below the last pitch. I began to jumar for the crest, but exhaustion and the difficult terrain slowed me to a crawl. My hands became numb from gripping the cold metal jumars so tightly; I couldn't feel my toes. Toward the top, my pack got stuck in a snow chimney and it took me time and effort to free it. Several yards below the top, the rope had cut deeply into the cornice and, no matter how I tried, I couldn't get my jumars to slide up any farther. Fighting for every inch, digging deeper into the crest with each struggle, I finally released my jumars, throwing my body over the lip and onto the flat slope above.

It was almost dark. Looking back along the route, I couldn't see Jim or Lou. The storm had quieted; there was less wind but now night was almost upon us.

I dropped my load and walked up the ridge a hundred yards in search of a campsite but found nothing large enough for a tent. Ten yards below, where I crested onto the ridge, seemed to be the only place. The site, sloping at twenty degrees, was only one yard away from the Northwest Face. It was the only place I could see that was wide enough to accept a tent. I started excavating a tent platform, first with my hands, then by sitting and pushing the snow away with my feet.

Once the platform was leveled, I pitched the large two-man Eddie Bauer tent. Jim had not come over the lip yet, but as I finished in the dark he struggled into view, having had the same problem with the upper five feet I had. He was totally exhausted and lay still in the snow.

"Have you seen Lou?"

"He's at the bottom of this rope," Jim gasped.

"Lou! Hey, Lou! Start up!"

I heard a faint but affirmative reply. Jim yelled to Lou to tie into the extra rope he had hauled. Jim belayed Lou up the difficult jumar.

I entered the tent and took off my boots while talking with Jim about his trouble on the way up. His description would have scared the others into leaving the mountain. Lou finally appeared out of the dark and both he and Jim set their packs near the tent and crawled inside. We all lay quietly for several minutes.

"That's the heaviest load I've ever carried on a mountain," Lou mumbled.

The tent became a mess as clothing, sleeping bags, and cooking gear were pulled from our packs. I started melting snow as soon as everyone had settled down, but Lou accidentally kicked the pot over just as all the snow had melted. There was a sudden mad scramble to keep sleeping bags and clothing dry. Jim found a sponge in the tent kit and soon things were back to normal. Over dinner we agreed to start for the summit the next day. We didn't want to stay any longer than necessary.

Lou radioed to Camp III at 7:00 P.M.

"We read you Lou," Willi responded. "How did everything go?"

Lou recounted the difficulties of the jumar and our late arrival to Camp IV. Willi was pleased with our progress. We made arrangements to talk again early the next morning. Jim took over the melting of snow after dinner and continued to keep all three of us supplied with hot liquids for several hours. At eleven o'clock the stove was turned off and we sacked out in the cramped but cozy tent.

It was the morning of September 1. "Camp Three," I called.

"Read you, John," Willi answered. "How are things up there this morning?"

"Fine, Willi, but we've decided to relax and hydrate today. We won't be moving."

Lou moved to the forward vestibule to cook breakfast while Jim and I relaxed, munching cornuts and candy.

"Certainly looks nice out there this morning," Lou observed, squinting into the sun. "No wind at all."

I leaned out the back of the tent. The skies were crystal clear and I noticed an unusual stillness in the air. "You know . . . maybe we better go for it with a day this calm."

"Do we have time?" Jim asked. "It's almost eight o'clock."

"Let's give it a try," Lou replied.

The tent became a madhouse. The stove was snuffed out with a flick of the wrist. We gulped down a warm milk-and-sugar drink Jim insisted we take before leaving. We scrambled for boots and clothes and were moving by 8:30 A.M.

I broke trail through the knee-deep sugar snow to a saddle several hundred yards above camp. Then Lou took over. He had been slow so far and had voiced his irritation at being tugged on several times. Lou continued slowly through the deep snow and up the corniced ridge to where it suddenly steepened. He surmounted a small rock problem and struggled above in waist-deep, baseless sugar snow. The terrain was terrible, sloping at fifty degrees and threatening to avalanche any moment. Lou slowed to a stop halfway up the slope. The altitude and deep snow were relentless antagonists.

I struggled to within a few feet of Lou, then took over the lead, moving steadily toward the top of the slope two hundred feet away. Soon I was pulling on Lou again; I didn't want to stay on that slope any longer than necessary.

"Goddamn it!" Lou burst out. "Stop pulling or I'm untying."

"Don't do that, Lou. I'll try not to pull on you from here."

He retied his knot and continued following in a

swimming motion. Soon the three of us were together on a small hump on the ridge.

"Your turn, Jim."

Jim moved on silently through the same waist-deep sugar along a knife crest. He stopped abruptly. "There's a small rock problem for John," he called over his shoulder.

"What do you mean?" I asked.

"You'll see." He turned and continued.

He surmounted the twenty-foot fluted gendarme and disappeared on the other side while Lou began to follow. I came last. After several of the gendarmes I was beside Jim and could see what he was referring to. Directly above him was a thirty-foot, black, horizontal rock band that mushroomed from the bottom up. Only to the right side, which dropped steeply over the Northwest Face, did there seem a climbable route. We had no rock hardware for use as protection.

"Get a better belay Jim," I said tensely. He was too far from the difficult section and his belay looked poor. I needed to attack the pitch quickly to eliminate any second thoughts, so I examined the pitch carefully while he prepared. Lou sat down twenty feet away and waited.

"Belay on?" I asked. Jim sensed my determination.

I chimneyed and jammed a short section before moving onto the face to overcome a short but difficult rock overhang. I followed another ice-and-rock gully, chimneying when possible, to above the band.

"I need more slack!"

Jim untied, giving me all I needed to wade and front point to the ridge crest above the rock band and place an acceptable belay.

"I'm up! Belay off!"

"Wait. Lou's decided not to go!" Jim shouted from below.

Lou was convinced by his altimeter that we had fifteen hundred feet still to go to the summit. If we went for the top, we would surely have to bivouac. He was not willing to take the chance of spending the night out without proper equipment. Lou also told Jim that he felt he had been forced against his will to ascend the Buttress the previous day; he was determined not to go against his better judgment this time.

"What do you think, Jim?" I yelled.

"I don't know. What do you think?" he yelled back.

"I'm going!" I shouted.

"I'm going too!" came Jim's reply.

Lou unroped and walked back along the ridge until he could see me. "We're not high enough! We've only gone five hundred vertical feet in four hours. I'm going back."

"By the shadow of Nanda Devi in the valley we're halfway!" I argued. "Your altimeter is wrong!"

"Good luck. I'll wait up for you in camp."

"O.K.—will you leave your parka with Jim?"

"No!"

"How about coming out to meet us with sleeping bags on our way down?"

"No! I'm not that altruistic," he replied.

I couldn't believe my ears. "O.K. Lou," I yelled. "Be careful on the way down. We're going on!"

Lou looked indecisive and angry. Jim and I got ready to continue. "All right, dammit, I'll come!"

"Good!" Jim replied with no hint of irritation.

They both made quick work of the rock band with tension from above. The next section appeared to be hard crampon snow but we were mistaken. Jim waded past and started breaking through the snow along a broad crest between two forty-five-degree slopes. What looked firm from below was in reality a heavy wind crust over bottomless powder. He floundered badly. The snow had no support and it required intense effort to move upward against the falling tide of heavy powder snow.

I broke for a stretch, then Lou did. No one had an easy time. The slopes on either side were heavy with fresh powder. Each move required throwing a knee up and over the crust to break it down, then falling forward with a swimming motion to gain a foot of distance.

I seemed to be able to move more efficiently and felt strong even while breaking, so I took the lead again. The avalanche conditions were extreme. Each time I put my hands in the snow in front of me, cracks raced across the slopes on either side. A loud hissing from the slope on my left drew my attention. I stopped wading and watched a two-foot-deep slab avalanche slide away, breaking from our tracks. Lou and Jim froze, silently watching the snow plummet into space over the Northeast Face several hundred feet below. I didn't think of the danger—strangely enough—but only of how unusual the scene was. It was as if I were watching the episode on TV. Lou's horrified look brought me back to reality. We had to get off this slope quickly.

I moved onto the crest's right side, which hadn't received any sun as yet, and dug furiously at the snow, making significant progress in height. The snow became belly deep, but I managed to plow through fast enough to start pulling on Lou and Jim struggling behind me. Again Lou became angry at being forced to move too fast and began to untie. I slowed down.

The snow conditions improved slightly to give us a base to move on. We topped out one by one onto a large open snowfield fifteen minutes after the avalanche. We moved together on a low-angled slope, Jim breaking trail in ankle-deep snow. The climbing was much easier. I led a stretch of steeper snow to a false summit and another expanse of lower-angled snow. After a brief discussion, we decided to have lunch on the slope. What we could see above might not be the summit.

Lou broke for a short distance after lunch, then Jim took the lead.

"That sure looks like a summit cornice," he said, approaching the overturned snow.

"Don't get your hopes up. It could be another false summit like the one below."

Jim stepped up and peered over the cornice.

"Do you see anything?" I asked excitedly.

"No!" he screamed, disappearing over the top. I followed closely and landed in a heap with Jim on the summit's other side. "This is it! We're here!" It was only 2:00 P.M.

Lou came over the crest. We grabbed one another, shaking hands and slapping shoulders.

The temperature was high enough for us to be comfortable. There was no wind. The weather had socked in below us and hid the surrounding peaks, including East Nanda Devi. We were able to remove our gloves and hats. Digging to the bottom of my pack, I brought out the American bicentennial flag and the Indian flag that we had been asked to take to the summit; Jim and Lou held them and beamed while I took pictures. Placing a flag inside an empty water bottle, I buried it deep in the summit snow. I couldn't have asked for better companions or a more magnificent ascent.

We sat comfortably, chatting about the expedition and the problems we had overcome to be there. Lou said he thought this was the best American climb since the West Ridge of Everest. I wondered if that team had faced similar problems, not knowing then that they had. After the months of preparation, difficulties within the team, and severity of route, it was hard to believe we were there.

Shortly after three o'clock we finished taking pictures, looked around us one last time, and descended single file into the clouds, through the deep trough of our ascent. Lou, the slowest, was first, then Jim, then me. I thought of our survival, my home, my family, our personal accomplishment. We were silent, each caught up in his own feelings. Although connected by one rope, we were in three different worlds.

We belayed the dangerous avalanche slopes and the rock band, then moved together down the steep bottomless snow to the rock step. Plunging forward, sometimes uncontrollably, we reached Camp IV by four o'clock.

THIRTEEN

Liquids were the first priority at Camp IV. We boiled pot after pot of water and drank deeply to rehydrate. Shadows deepened in the valleys while we savored a dinner of beef and vegetables. Lou reached Camp III on the radio at 5:30. "Devi! We took a rest day and climbed the nearest peak!"

"You went to the summit?"

"Yep, we were on top at two o'clock."

"Fantastic!" she cheered. "Congratulations on a wonderful job!" The rest of the team was returning from jumaring practice on the Buttress, so we agreed to talk with Willi at seven o'clock.

"Congratulations on your ascent," Willi's voice boomed over the radio. "We'll be sending a team up tomorrow to take your place—probably Devi, Peter, and Andy. Leave your sleeping bags at Camp Four and you can use theirs down here."

"John wants to know, what if they don't make it this far?" Lou asked. I didn't like the idea of being separated from my sleeping bag, but Lou later shamed me into agreement.

Andy's voice broke in: "Don't worry. We'll get there."

Hoping to get a good night's rest, Jim, Lou, and I slipped into our bags early. The altitude and crowded conditions, however, prevented us from sleeping very well. It was a long cold night after the summit.

We were awake at 6:00 A.M. It was too cold and too

early to descend. Jim leaned forward, still in his bag, and lit the stove. After a small breakfast with several cups of steaming tea, we dressed and left the tent to pack. Jim and I were gloveless; our Dachsteins (preshrunk woolen mittens made in Austria) were frozen solid, having become wet the day before. We held them against our bodies, straightened our gear, and waited for the sun to warm our tiny perch. The weather was beautiful.

I was too cold to wait very long, so I hooked my rappel system to the first rope, snapped a few pictures, and descended. Jim followed as soon as the rope went slack. I made it a point to wait at the end of each rope to take pictures of Jim rappeling and to make sure he was all right. Lou descended close behind. At Sugar Delight, I waited for half an hour for Jim to appear. He was coming down slowly, carefully. I stuffed an extra three-hundred-foot nine-millimeter rope and a rack of hardware I found at the anchor into my pack to take to Camp III, then, after seeing Jim round the corner, descended the rest of the Buttress.

Jim and I were at the base of the Buttress two hours after leaving Camp IV. "We're down!" We clasped each other's arms. "I couldn't feel my feet or hands on the first rappels—I thought I was going to lose them," he said. We relaxed in the snow and warm air and waited for Lou.

"I wonder where Devi, Andy, and Peter are?" Jim asked.

I was puzzled too. "On Dhaulagiri, someone would have broken trail out here to meet us. Usually someone's there . . ."

"They asked us to leave our gear at Four because they said they would be going up. And no one's gotten even this far. I can't understand why someone didn't meet us here at least—they know we're tired."

Lou descended the last rope to where we were sitting and removed his crampons. He, too, was disappointed not to see the second team. He was the one who had argued for us to leave our gear when the others insisted, and now he felt responsible. There was a single track fifty yards from Camp III where someone had ventured out that morning, but then decided against it and returned to camp. Jim had tears in his eyes. We stopped just behind a rise outside of camp to collect ourselves.

Kiran and Nirmal ran out of their tent to greet us warmly. John Evans and Peter came over and congratulated us. The others were more reserved, however. Although the proper words were spoken, it was a very cool welcome. By contrast, the air was quite warm; everyone gathered outside in the sun to discuss the route and the next few days. Devi passed around a pot of pink lemonade.

"Why didn't anyone go up today?" I asked after sitting down with the others.

"It looked like the weather would turn bad," Andy said.

"But it's been perfect all morning!"

"It looked bad earlier this morning. A large black cloud hung over Nanda Devi," he insisted. Andy later confided to Lou that Devi had not been feeling well, further influencing their decision not to go. Willi and the others began talking about going to Camp IV the next day.

"Who's on the second team, Willi?" I asked, hoping the team had been changed.

"Devi, Andy, and Peter."

I had great misgivings. "Willi, I'm going to say my piece."

"Yes, John, I thought you would," he said, laughing gently.

"I don't think Devi should go up, or Andy either, if he's still got that cough. Devi," I faced her, "you've got a hernia, which could give you problems, a bad cough you haven't shaken off since the expedition began, and you've been ill every other day from some stomach ailment. I think there are stronger people to go up—like Nirmal, or Evans. Willi could go with Peter. But neither you nor Andy have acclimatized."

They all looked right through me as if I were a phantom and not a man.

"That's it. I've said all I'm going to."

I expected to hear Jim or Lou back me up, but neither

said a word. I was alone in voicing what I thought was a serious problem.

Devi showed her anger with calculated subtlety. Since Base Camp, Jim had asked everyone—for health reasons—to use a clean utensil or cracker to scoop out the peanut butter. Devi thought this was a ridiculous rule, but obliged. Now she asked for the pail of peanut butter and opened it. Jabbing her fingers deep into the pail, she scooped out a glob of peanut butter and waved it in the air toward me. "*This* is the way we do it at Camp Three," she snapped, and ate from her fingers.

Several minutes later, Willi came over and we talked alone.

"I just don't think she should go up, Willi."

"Well John, what can a father do?"

"I don't know."

"What would you do if she were your daughter?"

"I don't know, Willi . . . she's not." Our conversation ended.

I finished unpacking while Willi went over to his tent to fix a jumar system for himself so that he could help on the Buttress the next day. The others had all disappeared into their tents. I was annoyed with Lou and Jim for not speaking up when I knew they believed in what I was saying, and I wanted to know why. Lou was in John Evans's tent. I went in and lay down beside him.

"Why didn't you back me up?"

"I guess I should have," Lou answered, but he had no explanation.

I found Jim in his tent, stretched out on a mat. As yet no one had offered us any sleeping bags for the night.

"Jim, why didn't you say something? You know Devi's got some health problems. They're not going to pay any attention to me."

"I don't think the hernia is that big a problem," he shrugged. "I haven't checked her out yet but I'll do that later this afternoon. Right now I don't have anything to go on."

Jim grew irritated with my questions, so I dropped the issue. No one wanted to argue with Willi. Dibrugheta and Marty's evacuation had been bad enough.

Meanwhile, Peter appeared outside our tent and peeked in. "Say, you guys want my sleeping bag? I'll be glad to let you have it."

We just about cried at Peter's offer. He had certainly changed in my eyes. "No, Peter, you need the rest if you expect to make it tomorrow. We'll do all right in down pants and coats," Jim said. "Could you loan us those?"

"Sure, I'll bring 'em right over." He turned to go.

"Say, Peter," I called impulsively. "Here's a bicentennial flag for you . . . Make sure you get it to the summit, O.K.?"

"Thanks, John," he smiled. "It'll get there."

That afternoon Jim did a short examination of Devi's hernia with Willi in attendance. "If she goes up, there's a chance of a problem," Jim concluded. "If the hernia strangulates and she develops pain in her abdomen, it will take about two hours to kill the bowel and up to two days to kill the patient." Devi and Willi accepted this.

With neither his own authority nor backing from Willi, the expedition leader, Jim could only warn them. "I didn't feel it was necessary to yell and scream," Jim told me later. "I knew Willi wouldn't take my advice, even though I told him I felt Devi shouldn't go up. He refused to take my advice at Dibrugheta on Marty's problem, even on a clear-cut medical issue. Devi's hernia was not clear cut; it was only problematic."

We spent the rest of the afternoon drinking and eating dinner that Devi prepared. That night, Jim and I dressed heavily in down coats and pants. Lou, having spilled his urine bottle inside his bag during our last night at Camp IV, had brought his sleeping bag down to dry out. It felt good not to have to trust those ropes again, and we dozed off.

September 3 was warmer than usual, and the weather looked promising. The powder snow squeaked under their boots as Andy and Devi left for the Buttress and Camp IV. Having left earlier, Peter was only a dot on the Ridge. Willi, Kiran, Nirmal, Evans, and Jatendra followed to practice jumaring behind the second summit team. Willi and the Indians were new to the technique;

John Evans, who was already experienced with jumars, would give them some pointers.

Only Lou, Jim, and I stayed behind, asleep in our tent, relaxing for the first time in days. We didn't have to ascend the Buttress again. I was concerned, though, for the others, knowing the difficulties they faced and the poor state of the fixed lines. Even the idea of practicing on the lower ropes made me nervous. The Buttress and upper slopes of Nanda Devi were socked in by drifting clouds, but we could monitor the second team's progress by listening to them calling to one another. The two parties seemed to spend a lot of time communicating. Jim, Lou, and I spent a leisurely day eating, relaxing, and listening to the climbers.

Jatendra, the only IMF trainee to reach Camp III, returned to camp first, exhausted by the hike from the Buttress. Willi, Kiran, Nirmal, and Evans returned several hours later, cold and tired. Practice on the ropes had not gone well. Willi and John had taught them what they could, but both Kiran and Nirmal had been too slow to reach Sugar Delight Snowfield. Jim cooked hot drinks for the returning climbers while Lou and I started dinner.

"Where did you last see the second team, Willi?" Lou asked.

"Andy was just below Devi and they were about to the snowfield," Willi guessed. "They were moving slowly."

There was no radio contact at 6:00 P.M., our scheduled time. We tried again at seven without success. Speculation as to what had happened spread among the tents. No one mentioned the possibility of the ropes breaking, but we all thought of it.

At 8:30 P.M., Peter came in over the radio from Camp IV. He sounded weak, and was probably hypothermic.

"O.K. Peter," Willi asked, "have you seen Devi or Andy?"

"I haven't seen them since four-thirty on Sugar Delight Snowfield. They were still coming, but slowly. Since then I've been working to get to here. It was a bitch."

"We want half-hour radio contacts until they both arrive, understand?" Willi ordered. "Hold on—Jim wants to speak with you."

"Heat up some milk and sugar, Peter," Jim instructed. "We left some in the pan in the front vestibule."

Peter came on again at 9:00 P.M. No one else had shown up yet, but his stronger voice indicated a definite improvement in his condition.

Willi was worried. He left the tent to yodel to Devi, their private mode of communication. Bell-like, his voice rang through the cold air, to be met only with silence. Then we heard Devi's faint, high-pitched reply. Her voice had cracked slightly; she was still alive.

Frozen and covered with snow, Andy arrived at Camp IV at 11:00 P.M. and piled into the tent with Peter. He had stayed behind Devi until Sugar Delight—where he had suggested turning back—but Devi had not taken the idea seriously. Andy continued staying just in front of Devi to keep an eye on her. She had a slow but even pace. He left her just below the ridge at the top of the gully and had managed to reach the crest. Devi should have been close behind.

Just before midnight, Lou thought he heard someone yell from the Buttress. It sounded like "Camp Three, Camp Three!" but he wasn't sure. Jim stepped outside in the clear starlit night and shone his headlamp at the Buttress, but there was no answer.

"Camp Three, Devi's here!" Peter finally reported.

Devi got the rope and jumars stuck fifteen feet below the crest, the place we all had had trouble. Unable to move up or down in her exhausted condition, she had yelled for help. We had heard her, but Peter and Andy, only thirty feet away and over the crest, hadn't heard a word. Worried about her taking so long, Andy returned to the crest, heard her yelling, and helped her up. The three of them were finally together and safe. It was 2:00 A.M. when they turned in to sleep. "There were many ominous signs . . . a very desultory start, poor weather, and Devi's hernia popped out," Lou wrote of their ascent in his diary. They had been lucky to get so far.

The next day, September 4, I was to descend to Base Camp and send a porter out to Lata to summon the rest of the porters we would need to leave the mountain. One of us had to go and I was the logical choice. As the only doctor, Jim would stay with the main group until everyone was down. Lou was torn between staying to help the summit team and leaving for the U.S. to be with his wife for the birth of their next child. We felt that all the climbers would summit in the next three or four days if everything worked out well. Already the second team was in position and the Indians needed only to perfect their jumar technique to follow a day or two later.

"We're not moving today," Andy told us at the morning radio call. "All of us need a day's rest. We're pretty tired."

"How's Devi?" Willi asked.

"Exhausted, but fine. Her hat fell off during her ascent yesterday, but we'll work something out."

I cooked rice pudding for breakfast, filled my water bottle, and packed to leave. Willi gave me last-minute instructions on how many porters to send for and where the money was hidden at Camp I. It was one of the finest days of the expedition and already, at 8:30 A.M., the air temperature was warm. Evans and I floundered through deep snow down the Ridge a short distance from camp to photograph the Buttress and upper slopes of Nanda Devi. At one point on the Ridge we could see Nanda Devi East. After saying my good-byes, I started down alone for Base Camp. The ropes were buried deep under a heavy crust of snow. Each step down was a difficult tug-of-war with the rope as I tried to free it from the mountain's icy grip. The load I was carrying, heavy with personal gear and ice hardware, kept throwing me off balance. My progress was almost as slow as it had been when I came up.

Camp II was a shambles after only three days. One of the tents was crushed from snowfall, the other in an equally bad condition. I searched through several opened food bags to find only cornuts and crackers. The sun was now viciously hot, pounding the snowfield and me along with it. I stripped some clothing along with my crampons, balled up with snow, and continued down to Camp I, weaving and jerking from side to side on each rappel. The arm pulling the rope from the crust was drained of strength and almost useless, so I let my body weight pull the rope free.

Camp I was deserted, silent. Tent doors flapped in the slight breeze; food bags were torn open and scattered. No one had been there for some time. I found Jim's film but not the expedition's money bag. I continued descending through the same snow conditions. At the end of the fixed lines I slid and punched my way through avalanche debris until I was just above Advanced Base. None of the debris had been there three weeks ago and I was amazed at the accumulation.

Dropping over a small cliff above Advanced Base, I rounded the hillside, expecting to see a lively camp with several of the high-altitude porters, but I was wrong. Before me were the ghostly skeletons of three tents. Only the poles were standing; wisely, the nylon tents had been dropped in case of avalanche blasts while the camp was empty. Like a victim of war, I scavenged the dead camp for food and the rest of the belongings I had left there a month before. Everything was wet and filthy. Ravens were digging at the garbage and food sacks, pecking apart the eight-man-day units.

The mountain was silent, the camp ghostly. I never felt so insignificant. Rummaging through an open box, I found a two-month-old *Newsweek* and read it through. Later I searched my duffel for personal gear and the exposed film I had left, dumping the climbing hardware from my pack to make room. It was almost as good as Christmas, finding gear I had forgotten was there.

It was 2:00 P.M., but I decided to continue down and across the glacier for Base because Advanced Base was too depressing. My pack made me sink in the snow at the side of the glacier, which I dreaded crossing. As I reached the side, I hesitated, then followed some several-day-old tracks until they disappeared under tons of avalanche debris. I didn't hurry. It was now or never and I didn't want to breathe hard or suck air. After ten minutes I was across. I hoped I would never have to cross that area again.

I passed through Ridge Camp quickly. Only a few torn boxes remained to indicate we had been there weeks before. I stayed to the side of another avalanche debris slope, then crossed where the stream had once been, now a trough of avalanche snow. An hour later I crossed the Rishi on an immense snow bridge. There was no more danger. I was down.

Dharamsingh, Kesharsingh, and Balbirsingh met me at the stream near camp. They were smiling and eager to help me across. Tears welled in my eyes when I saw them.

"Up, Sahib?" Dharamsingh asked excitedly.

"Yes, yes, all the way up!" I answered, gesturing. They shook my hand and insisted on taking the pack from my weary shoulders. I knew in my heart they shared our success. It was good to be with them again. That night in their company was one of the most pleasant I spent in India.

Jim and Lou had enjoyed an easy day at Camp III. Willi, Evans, Kiran, and Nirmal also spent the day in camp resting because they planned to attempt Camp IV the next day. Willi was still unsure whether the Indians could jumar the ropes and decided to get an early start the next morning.

Lou continued to worry about his wife Kathy. Jim persuaded him to leave for home the following day. There was no reason for Lou to stay; Jim would take his responsibilities.

No one had moved from Camp IV that day either. During the afternoon radio call Jim asked Devi about her hernia and about any symptoms of illness she may have had. Both Lou and Jim doubted she should go higher and Jim warned her about his concern.

"Willi, I only advised her to come down," Jim said. "I didn't order her."

"I'm glad you left it that way," Willi replied.

Before dawn on the fifth, Peter, Devi, and Andy at Camp IV were up and dressing. The weather was partly cloudy and a breeze was beginning to pick up. Devi was still lethargic and had some diarrhea. She decided to wait another day or until Willi could be with her to go for the summit. Andy complained of being tired and elected to stay with Devi. Peter wanted to go part way at least. He needed to make the attempt even if alone. His would be the expedition's last attempt for the summit.

Peter pushed hard, surmounting the major difficulties of the upper section, but turned back just below the rock band. The weather had worsened considerably as he climbed and snow began falling. He became exhausted in the deep snow and high altitude and, while descending, slipped and fell toward the abyss of the Northwest Face. Miraculously, he stopped after thirty feet, even though he had dropped his ice axe. After retrieving the axe, Peter descended more carefully and reached Camp IV in the afternoon. He retreated to the safety of the tent, where he, Devi, and Andy spent their third night at 24,000 feet.

At Camp III, Willi, Kiran, Nirmal, and Evans had gone through a similar day of hardship on the Buttress. The third summit team was awake at 6:00 A.M. and viewed the same storm clouds in the south, but decided to attempt the ascent of the Buttress anyway. After Jim fed them a hot breakfast, the four headed for the ropes and Camp IV. Jim and Lou descended: Jim for a food bag for Camp III, Lou for home. Jim returned to camp slowly, reaching the Ridge in a snowstorm. He relaxed the rest of the day, boiling liquids and listening to the climbers on the Buttress arguing whether to go up or down.

The four climbers straggled into camp at nine o'clock that night. Nirmal and Kiran had again been too slow; it was wiser to descend rather than try for Camp IV. John Evans, usually placid and introverted, was furious. "Willi purposely overextended the whole team," he told Jim. "We were in real danger."

The climbers were hypothermic, particularly Evans, and Jim forced foods and fluids into them. According to Evans, they were lucky to have made it back to camp alive.

For me, it was a peaceful September fifth. I sent all the porters to Advanced Base except Dharamsingh, who was to run to Lata for more porters, and Tesh, a porter who was ill. I bathed early, long before the sun's warmth arrived in the deep valley, then walked through the meadows. The sounds and smells of the valley pleased my senses. It was another world.

Fall had come to the upper Sanctuary. Frost covered the vegetation along the spring that flowed through camp. The bright plants and flowers, predominant in August, had faded and withered. I thought about the expedition as I walked along a sheep trail above camp. The team had never been together in spirit in the United States or on the mountain. We had been divided by philosophy and opinion since the beginning. Success under such circumstances seemed even sweeter. Yet I was worried deeply about those still trying to summit. Kiran scared me because he was irrational when it came to "saving face." I knew he was not technically proficient and his tenacity could cause himself and others trouble on the Buttress.

Now that she had overcome the difficulties of the Buttress, Devi worried me less. But her illness and hernia made me think that she would only reach Camp IV. Willi had said that she was used to an unusual amount of stomach trouble and carried her own antacid. Perhaps she could mask her discomfort long enough to summit.

The day passed quickly for me at Base. I felt sure that someone had reached the top that afternoon because of the good weather, although it looked windy near the summit. I was hoping they would get up and down quickly so we could leave for home.

Early the next morning, on the sixth, I walked up the hill above Base to photograph Nanda Devi. Clouds sped past the summit and the winds looked fierce. Lou was at Base when I returned at noon. We briefly wished each other success and he continued to Pathal Khan, loaded with all the Gumperts drink mix and *chapatis* Tesh and I could give him. He hadn't heard anything from the others at Camp IV, but assumed they must have made the summit. I was entertained the rest of the day by two Japanese who were in the Sanctuary scouting a route on the northeast side that would eventually reach the North Ridge and ascend our Buttress. It would be a difficult, magnificent route if they could do it. Unfortunately, they didn't succeed.

* * *

Both Camp III and IV were awake and busy at 6:30 A.M. Devi made the scheduled radio contact with Willi and Jim.

"I'm going alone to Camp IV," Willi announced. "Yesterday Kiran and Nirmal were too slow on the ropes. Kiran even ended up upside down trying to jumar." Kiran and Nirmal couldn't decide what they would do. Kiran thought of soloing to Camp IV like Willi, but Nirmal wanted to go down. Later, under pressure from Kiran, Nirmal changed his mind.

Evans was ambivalent. He was feeling very lethargic and had been sleeping constantly for the past twenty-four hours. Jim thought this was due to exhaustion and hypothermia from the previous day. He couldn't know Evans was coming down with hepatitis. Evans later decided to descend because he didn't want to guide Kiran and Nirmal up the Buttress and to the top. Willi left for Camp IV shortly after breakfast.

That day the three climbers at Camp IV again remained in camp. Peter was exhausted from his solo attempt and needed the rest. Andy's desire to summit now depended solely on Devi; he'd do whatever she decided.

In the weeks on the upper slopes of Nanda Devi, Andy had asked for Devi's hand in marriage, and Willi had given his blessing. They would set a date when they returned home. The rest of us didn't know of their intended marriage. They didn't know what our reaction would be and, frankly, didn't care. The engagement was their secret and comfort during a very difficult time on the mountain.

In the meantime, the mountain had taken second place for Andy. His affection for Devi preempted his previous goals. Before he and Devi had gone up the Buttress, Andy had told her that no mountain was worth the risk, that instead he wanted to "wrap her in cotton wool." They both laughed at this and agreed that wasn't what Devi wanted or needed. She promised to tell him if she had the slightest inkling of trouble.

Andy retrieved the rope below Camp IV that morning. Devi felt lethargic, as she had since her arrival, so they performed a little test to see how strong she was. She climbed about thirty feet out of camp, stopped, rested, then returned. Devi was simply exhausted for no apparent reason. Although she still had diarrhea that morning, she seemed fine as long as she wasn't moving.

At the two o'clock radio call, Jim informed Camp IV that Willi was on his way up and that they should dig another tent platform. Jim knew Devi was a stoic about illness and pleaded with her, "Devi, what aren't you telling me?"

"I'm telling you everything," she answered. "I have no pain."

Later in the day Andy, Peter, and Devi decided she should descend. According to Andy: "Nothing suggested urgency, just her lassitude and diarrhea." Andy and Peter dug another tent site, but the wind prevented them from pitching a tent. Because Willi was on his way, they decided not to escort Devi down that afternoon.

He arrived around 7:00 P.M. He had never used a jumar in his life, yet had accomplished one of the most difficult jumars a climber would ever encounter. Willi, Peter, and Andy decided to climb to the summit early the next morning. They would take Devi down upon their return. That night, Devi had terrible sulfur burps and complained of being cold and clammy.

High winds and snow pinned those at Camp IV down on September 7. The four had no choice but to sit out the storm. They made the best of a poor situation, cooking meals and boiling water to stay healthy. Devi's abdomen was tender and slightly distended, but the hernia appeared to be in place. She continued taking plenty of liquids and food. Toward evening, she again had severe sulfur burps and diarrhea. The others watched her carefully, although nothing suggested urgency to them.

"She ought to come down," Jim told Willi that evening. "Sounds to me as though she's getting some bowel obstruction."

"No, she has heartburn," Willi said. "Someone should bring up an antacid tomorrow."

Meanwhile, the climbers at Camp III sat out the bad day as well. Nirmal had complained of leg pains, acute chest pain, and shortness of breath, and Jim began to suspect a possible pulmonary embolism. His main concern now was Evans, who was revealing some real problems that Jim wasn't sure of. Jim evacuated both men with the help of Kiran and Jatendra the next morning.

Bad weather continued on September 8. The night at Camp IV had been difficult. The four occupants of the two-man tent had been cramped. Devi's condition was markedly worse.

Her sulfur burps were more frequent; she had to be helped into a sitting position, the only position she was able to assume with any degree of comfort. Andy had felt Devi's abdomen and it had become severely distended. The hernia was in place but she was in pain. They discussed the situation and decided, in spite of the bad weather, to help her down that morning.

Devi's burps became constant and her cheeks were puffy. Her face and lips took on a blue hue. At 10:00 A.M., according to Peter, she looked bad and everyone was concerned. Her face became puffier and puffier. The vicious storm, worse than any since we had arrived in the Sanctuary, delayed their departure until noon.

Willi went outside, leaving the others to put on their clothes and ready themselves to descend. Devi was sitting up in the back of the tent trying to drink some cocoa. Her stomach hurt terribly.

Devi suddenly became a ghostly white. "Take my pulse Peter," she said. Then, calmly, "I'm going to die." Her eyes rolled as she pitched forward and vomited.

Andy grabbed her and started mouth-to-mouth resuscitation. Peter called Willi back into the tent. Willi immediately took over the mouth-to-mouth while all three tried cardiopulmonary resuscitation.

Willi would recall he knew they had lost her within fifteen minutes as he felt her lips grow cold against his. They continued their efforts to revive her for another half hour without success. The three men were anguished. Devi was dead.

They clasped each other for comfort as their quiet moans filled the tent. What could they do with Devi's body? Leave her in the tent? Bury her?

"No," Willi decided. "We will commit her to the mountain. As if a burial at sea."

Stricken, Willi, Peter, and Andy finished dressing. Hugs and touches consumed their last moments with Devi. The sleeping bag was zipped shut and the drawstring closed around her face. Then into the raging storm they crawled.

They dragged her body up the ridge a short distance. It was to the uphill side of the fixed lines so that her remains would find their way into the most remote icy grave on Nanda Devi—the Northeast Face. They fell to their knees in the storm and linked their hands in a circle around her corpse. Each sobbed a broken farewell to the comrade who had filled such a vivid place in their lives. Willi said last rites:

"Thank you for the world we live in. Thank you for such beauty juxtaposed against such risk . . . Thank you."

The three men dragged Devi to the edge of the face. With a horrible shove, her corpse disappeared into the bowels of the storm, into the mountain of the Goddess Nanda Devi.

"We laid the body to rest in its icy tomb, at rest on the breast of the bliss-giving Goddess Nanda," Willi later pronounced.

Now cold and exhausted, their judgment distorted by grief, the climbers knew one thing: they had to leave Camp IV immediately.

An hour elapsed as they packed and readied to descend in the raging storm. Willi packed only those items of Devi's dearest to him. Peter and Andy descended first. Neither made the swing-over into the gully easily. Peter, already emotionally drained, felt as though the rope were strangling him. It eventually squeezed him so tight he thought he would die.

Willi drove himself beyond the limits of most men. Never have I met a man so determined. At times he asked himself if he even wanted to continue, yet each time he struggled on. The traverse from the gully to Sugar Delight almost decided for him. Because of the small ledge and unanchored section of rope, it was the most difficult section to descend. Each step of the traverse along the eight-inch ledge pushed the climber away from the wall. Balance was essential.

Willi slipped off the ledge and started to strangle. He knew he was in a struggle for his life. There was only one choice he could make to survive. He had to get rid of his pack and, with it, Devi's keepsakes. With extreme effort, Willi managed to hook the pack to the rope, hand-line to the anchor, and pull himself to safety. He wrenched himself away from the traverse and continued down. Once he dropped a glove and froze several fingers. Somehow he connected each rappel correctly, following Peter and Andy down the ropes in the black of night. Sometime during the night all three reached the base of the Buttress. Exhausted and close to the limit of survival, they arrived at 10:00 P.M.

The four sahibs and one porter there had descended to Advanced Base. Kiran and Jatendra escorted Nirmal, who had chest pains, while Jim stayed with Evans, now lethargic and slow. He was exhibiting symptoms of hepatitis and had to descend quickly.

There had been no radio contact between the two groups of climbers until late in the night, when Andy, Peter, and Willi finally called Jim at Advanced Base. Only then did the other team members learn of Devi's death.

"You had better stay at Camp III tomorrow and rest," Jim suggested. Lamely he added, "We're all terribly sorry, Willi."

FOURTEEN

Down at Base, I was worried. Someone should have been with me by now. I was sure that Kiran had gone too far, hurting himself or somebody else. Or maybe it was Devi. When no one arrived at Base the night of September 10, I knew there had been trouble.

On the morning of the eleventh, I sent a note to Advanced Base with Surrendra, asking for a reply from any sahib there. That night a porter returned with a radio and a note from Willi with instructions for a radio call at six o'clock. I was to move away from the camp so no one could hear the conversation.

At six, I walked several hundred yards above camp and made contact. I knew instinctively his news would be bad, and tried to prepare myself.

"John, are you alone?" Jim asked over the radio.

"Yes."

"Willi has something to say."

"John . . . we lost Devi," Willi said, his voice cracking.

A numbing sensation crept over me. "I'm very sorry, Willi . . . is there anything I can do?"

"No. We committed her body to the mountain."

I didn't want to ask how she died and Willi didn't offer the reason.

"Do you want me to go back up and get her?"

"No. Thanks, though," his voice cracked again. "That's impossible now. We barely made it down ourselves. I had to leave Devi's pack on the Buttress to save myself."

"I'll go up and get the pack for you."

"No. I don't want anybody going back up there."

"I'm really sorry, Willi," I said again. "I'll wait for your call tomorrow morning."

"One more thing, John," he asked. "I don't want this to reach the porters yet."

Most of the sahibs arrived at Base Camp on September 12. I waited impatiently for someone, but it wasn't until midafternoon that I saw a figure cross the Rishi. It was Jatendra. Haggard and loaded with gear, he could only say how sorry he was that Devi had died.

Jim appeared an hour later. I met him at the creek just outside of Base. Tears welled up in our eyes and we embraced. I took his pack and we walked back to camp.

John Evans and Peter arrived next, exhausted. Evans's hepatitis had caused his eyes to become sunken and turn a sickly yellow. The sun had turned his lips into black scabs. Peter came over to me immediately after dumping his pack.

"I think the route is fantastic—there are only a handful of climbers who could have led that Buttress. And here's the bicentennial flag you gave me," he added. "I'm sorry I didn't get it to the summit."

He then sat down and described the entire incident concerning Devi from start to finish. I found it hard to believe that she had died so suddenly and mysteriously.

We fell asleep late in the night. Our plan was to send some of the porters to Advanced Base in the morning to retrieve gear still on the mountain. Kiran and Willi, still at Advanced Base, would see to it that everything was removed and the trash burned.

Early that afternoon, Dharamsingh burst into camp with porters and the all-important mail from home. Although written over a month before, each piece of news was eagerly read and shared.

The first high-altitude porters and Nirmal arrived from Advanced Base in the afternoon, heavily laden with gear. They brought unexpected good news. Everyone was coming down with double loads, upwards of seventy pounds, so the mountain would be clean at last. We could plan on leaving the Sanctuary the next day.

Willi shuffled into camp, walking like a wounded soldier. It was too painful for him to walk on his toeless feet, which had been damaged again with frostbite during his retreat from Camp IV. He shuffled along on the sides of his feet, then hobbled where the going was better. Kiran had donated a large pair of Indian Army tennis shoes to Willi, which were only half-filled because of his missing toes.

Two cables were immediately dispatched from Base Camp with Dharamsingh. The first was sent to Jolene, Willi's wife. The cable read:

"Devi died 8 Sept Camp IV Acute Mountain Sickness. Body committed to mountain. Out of beauty into beauty."

The second cable was sent to H. C. Sarin, president of the Indian Mountaineering Federation. It explained the death and that we were departing the Sanctuary.

One evening during dinner, Andy and Willi discussed the tragedy at Camp IV. Based on their description, Jim offered a late diagnosis of what may have killed Devi: an acute abdominal disorder complicated by altitude.

Willi asked for our cooperation in handling the press when we reached New Delhi. We agreed and went to sleep. That night was the first night of the entire trip that Willi and I shared the same tent.

The peacefulness of Lata was shattered as porters and sahibs arrived laden with gear and tired from the long journey. It had taken only three days from Base Camp. Tea and biscuits were served at each house as we were treated to each porter's hospitality and observed the proper protocol for VIPs.

Late in the afternoon we climbed above the village to the Shrine of Nanda Devi and were joined there by the many village men. Women were not allowed near the shrine. Dominating the grounds was the Temple of the Goddess Nanda Devi, which looked out upon the village and deep valley beyond. The priest of the village unlocked several doors of iron and wood that lead to the shrine, then beckoned us to move closer and look inside.

Willi and the priest entered first. They were by themselves several minutes before we humbly walked inside to view the goddess's image and her earthly possessions. We were required to remove our footwear before entering, beneath a stone archway, the temple grounds. The small courtyard of flagstone was surrounded on two sides by one-story stone buildings with tiny cubicles inside.

Candles cast an eerie light on a distorted mannequin in a woman's image with stringy hair, a large mouth, and wide eyes. It was dressed gaudily in ornate cloth and brass ornaments. Cloth, bowls, brass figures, and spears adorned the room. Several large knives were leaning against the walls; the priest let us examine them thoroughly while Balbirsingh translated for us.

Along with the priest and Willi, we bowed and prayed for Devi and the Goddess Nanda, then were escorted outside. Willi remained alone, briefly. He came out minutes later, tears in his eyes. A goat, to be sacrificed to the Goddess Nanda, was lead into the courtyard. One man held him by a tether while another villager sprinkled water on the animal to get him to shake his body from head to tail. With one blow of the fifteen-pound blade, its head was lopped off. The priest spotted its blood on our foreheads and the rite was over.

With porters paid in Lata Kharak, we headed through Joshimath, Chomoli, and Rishikesh on the swaying buses spewing black diesel smoke. We arrived at the YMCA in New Delhi at four o'clock in the morning, checked into two-person rooms, and went to sleep. My eyes hurt badly and the surrounding eye muscles could not control their operation, a sign of what would become spinal meningitis. After several hours of sleep, we showered and met for breakfast. Willi called for our attention.

"Mr. Sarin, president of the Indian Mountaineering Federation, called and has arranged a news conference early this afternoon," Willi began. "We need to organize all the equipment that's going to be given to the IMF and take it with us for presentation to Sarin. That's everything, except I would like Jim and me to answer any questions about Devi's death, if that's O.K." We all agreed.

We spent the morning packing the personal gear to take home with us, as well as the group gear that was to be shipped by boat. Once done with the team chores, we scoured the streets of New Delhi for souvenirs to take home to our families. Our flight was due to leave that evening.

Mr. Sarin picked us up at the hotel with several vehicles at noon and escorted us to the IMF building, where the news conference was to be held. The team sat behind a conference desk and microphones, while Sarin, Willi, and Jim answered the pointed questions about the expedition and Devi's death. At the end of the press conference, Willi explained Devi's death in his own words: "Nanda Devi died doing the thing she loved best," he said. "She died fulfilling her dreams, out of her enormous love for the high Himalayas. She now lies in an eternal part of her namesake."

Our attempt to leave India that night failed because our papers from Chomoli were incomplete. With help from Mr. Sarin the next day, the papers were properly filed. We left India on the first flight from New Delhi on the night of September 19.

Our Indian companions gave us a poignant interpretation of Devi's death. According to them, when Willi Unsoeld announced in 1949 that he would name his daughter after the most beautiful mountain he had ever seen, the Goddess Nanda was later reborn as his daughter. She lived for some years as a mortal, unaware of her divine nature. She was instrumental in organizing the expedition that brought her home.

"Devi lives; she has not died," wrote one of the Indian members of the expedition. "She was the goddess personified."

Why Devi? She had more life bursting from her than did ten of us. Had she been too set on reaching the summit even with the physical problems she was having? Could she be blamed for pushing ahead regardless of her symptoms? Was she prepared for the difficulties of the climb?

Devi did what any one of us would have under the circumstances. With vague and intermittent symptoms, any of us would have chosen to proceed. And why not? She felt fine most days. On only one out of every four days did she suffer from symptoms of *Giardia*, a parasite in the intestines, and seldom did her hernia extend during the trip. She had climbed to Camp III without any obvious trouble, although jumaring the ropes to Camp IV was much more physically demanding than any other part of the mountain.

It was not Devi's nature to quit. She had inherited Willi's indomitable tenacity and drive, traits that had made her the best at whatever she attempted. One would have to conclude Devi played the game like a professional and simply lost. The expedition was over for most of us when we returned to the United States. But for Willi, the Nanda Devi expedition probably never ended until his own death in 1979, on Mt. Rainier.

The expedition changed us all. Devi is still carrying out her life's work in the hearts of everyone she had touched; now it is her spirit that moves us, although no longer her smile and understanding. I believe Devi's existence has changed us. I know she has widened my outlook on life.

EPILOGUE

Ten long years have erased a lot of my memories. Trails that I once followed into remote Shangri-las are less distinct. Mountains whose sharp ridges and dark north faces once challenged my very being I now remember softly, like a faded watercolor painting. Climbers with whom I shared danger, pain, and laughter have succumbed to age and respectability, and sometimes death. So many of the events that I thought would never leave my mind have slipped away without even a parting farewell—with one exception. I have not forgotten Nanda Devi.

Recalling the expedition to the "Goddess of Joy" is still painful for me: What joy is there in death? In laying bare others' weaknesses? In the frailty of our wisdom? There is none. Nowadays my wife Joyce won't allow me to dwell on Nanda Devi because she knows, once begun, I can't control the futility that grips me as I question over and over the decisions that led to the tragedy there.

The climbers who challenged Nanda Devi in 1976 have all changed with the years—those, of course, who are still alive. Of the thirteen climbers who shared their dreams that summer, four have died, taken by the mountains that all of them loved. Devi, Willi, Marty, and Kiran are gone.

Nanda Devi and the Sanctuary were made into an Indian National Park in 1982 and closed to further mountaineering and trekking. It was an intelligent move by the Indian government to prevent continued ecological destruction of the area. When it will be reopened to selected expeditions is unknown.

Those of us who are still alive are not friends so much as fellow prisoners of the same memories. The passage of time has eased the tension, but our eyes don't meet and our conversation is hurried and short. What happened on Nanda Devi could have happened to any group of people. But it happened to us; it was our tragedy and not one of us can explain why. Mountain climbers are usually so reserved, so exact. No one of us expected our differences of opinion to lead to death.

APPENDIX

Significant Dates of the 1976 Indo-American Nanda Devi Expedition

5 July: Leave Spokane and the United States
6 July: Arrive in New Delhi, India
9 July: Depart from New Delhi
14 July: Depart from Lata; first day of trek
16 July: Marty falls ill
17 July: Marty evacuated to Dibrugheta
19 July: Main group departs for next trek camp
22 July: Marty evacuated by helicopter; arrival at Base Camp
24 July: Lou and John occupy Ridge Camp
29 July: Lou, Jim, and John occupy Advanced Base Camp
22 August: Lou and John make the Ridge and establish Camp III
26–29 August: John leads the Buttress with Jim and Lou as partners
31 August: Lou, Jim, and John occupy Camp IV at top of Buttress
1 September: Fifth ascent of Nanda Devi; summit achieved by Lou, Jim, and John
3 September: Devi, Andy, and Peter reach Camp IV
8 September: Devi dies at Camp IV
14 September: Expedition leaves Base Camp
16 September: Arrive in Lata
22 September: Return to Spokane, Washington

JOHN ROSKELLEY is one of the world's foremost mountaineers. He has, in over twenty years' climbing experience, scaled the highest, most difficult peaks on earth. Roskelley has climbed more Himalayan peaks than any other American, including ascents of K2, Makalu, and Dhaulagiri. In 1974, he and partner Chris Kopczynski made the first American team-ascent of the infamous North Face of Switzerland's Eiger.

Roskelley lives in Spokane, Washington, with his wife and two children. This is his first book.